THE COMPLETE ILLUSTRATED GUIDE TO

COIN

COLLECTING

THE COMPLETE ILLUSTRATED GUIDE TO

COIN COLLECTING

How to start and build a great collection: the complete companion to world coins from antiquity to the present day, including 750 colour photographs

Tips on identification, authentication, coin care, presentation, cataloguing, buying and selling, plus how to plan and organize your collection as it grows

Dr James Mackay

southwater

This edition is published by Southwater

Southwater is an imprint of Anness Publishing Ltd
Hermes House, 88–89 Blackfriars Road, London SE1 8HA
tel. 020 7401 2077; fax 020 7633 9499
www.southwaterbooks.com; www.annesspublishing.com

Anness Publishing has a new picture agency outlet for publishing, promotions and advertising. Please visit our
website www.practicalpictures.com for more information.

UK agent: The Manning Partnership Ltd, 6 The Old Dairy, Melcombe Road,
Bath BA2 3LR; tel. 01225 478444; fax 01225 478440; sales@manning-partnership.co.uk

UK distributor: Grantham Book Services Ltd, Isaac Newton Way, Alma Park Industrial Estate, Grantham,
Lincs NG31 9SD; tel. 01476 541080; fax 01476 541061; orders@gbs.tbs-ltd.co.uk

North American agent/distributor: National Book Network, 4501 Forbes Boulevard, Suite 200, Lanham,
MD 20706; tel. 301 459 3366; fax 301 429 5746; www.nbnbooks.com

Australian agent/distributor: Pan Macmillan Australia, Level 18, St Martins Tower, 31 Market St, Sydney,
NSW 2000; tel. 1300 135 113; fax 1300 135 103; customer.service@macmillan.com.au

New Zealand agent/distributor: David Bateman Ltd, 30 Tarndale Grove, Off Bush Road, Albany, Auckland; tel.
(09) 415 7664; fax (09) 415 8892

ETHICAL TRADING POLICY

A CIP catalogue record for this book is available from the British Library.

Publisher: Joanna Lorenz
Editorial Director: Helen Sudell
Project Editor: Catherine Stuart
Production Controller: Wendy Lawson
Designer: Nigel Partridge and Balley Design
Photographer: Mark Wood

10 9 8 7 6 5 4 3 2 1

NOTE

Every effort has been made to reproduce coins at their actual size. However, readers should treat the images of
coins in the book as representative of dimensions, rather than actual size. Some coins have been enlarged or
reduced slightly to make some of the features more legible, but such modifications have been kept to a minimum.

The illustration on page 2 shows coiners at work in Germany during the 16th century.

CONTENTS

INTRODUCING COINS AND NUMISMATICS

In his First Epistle to Timothy, St Paul declared that the love of money was the root of all evil. Clearly, he did not have numismatists (as coin collectors like to style themselves) in mind. Were there coin collectors back in the 1st century? Quite possibly, for the design and production of coins had risen to a very high level by that time and today we regard the Greek coins of the late pre-Christian era as some of the most exquisite works of art ever produced.

In St Paul's day the coins of the early Roman Empire were already showing their character, with accurate likenesses of emperors and their families on one side and generally a female figure representing some abstract concept such as Justice, Concord or Agriculture on the other. From the relatively large numbers of classical coins that have

survived in fine condition it must be assumed that wealthy Greeks and Romans were laying aside beautiful specimens to admire rather than spend. Certainly, by the Renaissance in the 15th century, princes and magnates had their coin cabinets, and it was the appreciation of classical coins that inspired the revolution in coin design and production from the 1450s.

Today the role of coins in everyday life is being supplanted by plastic in the form of credit cards and cash cards. There is a popular anecdote about a little boy who went into a grocery store, picked up a packet of ice cream and at the checkout proffered a used telephone card as payment. He had often seen his mother handing over something similar, which was accepted instead of cash. This story indicates

Above: New Zealand 3 pence of 1946 with a portrait of George VI and a reverse motif of Maori war clubs.

how a generation of children are growing up more accustomed to plastic than metal – they may never experience the tactile pleasure of jingling a handful of coins in their pockets.

Despite this gradual narrowing of the actual usage of metal money, coins as collectables have developed dramatically. Not only are the mints and treasuries of the world producing more and more deluxe items for collectors, but the coins in general circulation are more varied than at any time since the fall of the Roman Empire. For centuries coin collecting was the preserve of the upper classes, who had the wealth to indulge their passion, as well as the classical education to appreciate the designs and inscriptions. Today coin collecting is a hobby pursued by people of all ages and incomes.

STARTING A COLLECTION

A good place to begin is at home, with the small change in daily circulation. The collection can very quickly be extended to past issues of your own country, often readily available from local coin dealers, and then to the coins of related territories. These may be similar in denomination and appearance, but the coins of every country are distinctive, such as the 1946 silver 3 pence of New Zealand shown above, with the profile of George VI on one side, just like the British coins, but a pair of Maori war clubs on the other.

The names and nicknames of coins can give clues to their history. The American quarter dollar is still referred

Above: An interesting coin of ancient Rome featuring a serrated edge and a sacrificial bull ritual on the reverse.

Below: This 1st-century relief shows the kind of money bag a travelling moneyer would have taken to a Roman treasury.

Above: An early Roman coin showing Apollo (left) on the obverse side. Later, portraits of emperors replaced deities.

Below: Coining is entwined with metal craft. The Gold Weigher, *by Dutch artist Gerard Dou, appeared in 1664.*

to as a two-bit coin, but few realize that the bit was originally the eighth part of a Spanish dollar, the *peso a ocho reales* (or "piece of eight" in pirate lore). The dollar sign ($) itself is a relic of this – it was originally a figure 8 with two vertical strokes through it.

Coins are usually identified by their inscription, and sometimes the denomination is helpful. Ancient coins are more of a problem; in the absence of any lettering, the effigy or emblem may be the only clue to identity. Where inscriptions exist and are legible, you can look for dates or the mint-marks identifying the place where the coins were struck. For example, American coins found without a mint-mark indicate that they were struck at the US Mint in Philadelphia, while those produced at the branch mints in Denver and San Francisco bear an initial letter D or S alongside the date.

The current range of American coins may seem limited – effectively the only coins in everyday use are the bronze cent (penny), 5 cents (nickel), 10 cents (dime) and 25 cents (quarter) – but in any handful of change you will find different dates and mint-marks. It is not

Below: A page from an American coin album designed to house Lincoln cents of each date and mint-mark.

The 1989 U.S. Mint Uncirculated Set

surprising, therefore, that coin collecting at its most basic, known by many as change-checking, should have developed into a national pastime in the United States.

This has led companies to produce a variety of housing options, such as albums of stout card pages with holes punched out to take the entire range of a particular denomination. The holes are annotated with the dates and mint-marks, and this encourages people to look for all the date and mark varieties.

Sooner or later you may want to start trading your coins, to finance new purchases and get rid of those in which you have less interest. Today there are many on-line businesses devoted to the sale of coins, while coin fairs – national and local – are great occasions to meet collectors and learn about your coins.

THE TRUE VALUE OF COINS

There are many opportunities nowadays to expand a coin collection at little cost, and the inclusion of related, non-coin items contributes colour, variety and context. My first trip abroad was to Greece in 1950, where there were no coins at all, just ragged paper printed with lots of noughts, reflecting the horrendous inflation of the immediate post-war years. In early 1950s, Holland I handled my first real foreign coins, but also saw massive silver 2½ gulden coins worn as buttons on the traditional jackets of Dutch men.

Above: Many mints now sell complete year sets, attractively packaged.

Rare vintage coins may sell for enormous sums, but most coins have a value of a different nature. When my father uncovered various copper coins of George III's reign in our garden, I took them to the local museum. The curator opined that someone, perhaps a farm labourer, had probably dropped his purse. Although I was disappointed to learn that the coins were very common and virtually worthless, I got a tremendous thrill imagining that they were the hard-won earnings of some poor ploughboy 150 years earlier. Today, when I handle a chunky Alexandrine tetradrachm of the 4th century BC I still get that tactile thrill, thinking that self-same piece of silver was earned, handled and spent by someone almost 2400 years ago.

Above: The reverse of a Netherlands 2½ gulden of William II, shown at actual size. These coins were often mounted and worn as buttons by Dutch people.

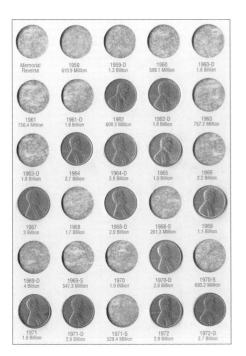

Memorial Reverse	1959 610.9 Million	1959-D 1.3 Billion	1960 588.1 Million	1960-D 1.6 Billion
1961 756.4 Million	1961-D 1.8 Billion	1962 609.3 Million	1962-D 1.8 Billion	1963 757.2 Million
1963-D 1.8 Billion	1964 2.7 Billion	1964-D 3.8 Billion	1965 1.5 Billion	1966 2.2 Billion
1967 3 Billion	1968 1.7 Billion	1968-D 2.9 Billion	1968-S 261.3 Million	1969 1.1 Billion
1969-D 4 Billion	1969-S 547.3 Million	1970 1.9 Billion	1970-D 2.9 Billion	1970-S 693.2 Million
1971 1.9 Billion	1971-D 2.9 Billion	1971-S 528.4 Million	1972 2.9 Billion	1972-D 2.7 Billion

WHAT ARE COINS?

Pieces of metal stamped with a device guaranteeing their worth developed more or less simultaneously in China and Asia Minor (modern Turkey) in the 7th century BC. Generally round and flat, modern coins may have different designs and inscriptions but are akin to the coins used centuries ago, like this 12th-century copper 10 cash of the Chinese Song dynasty.

THE HISTORY OF BARTER

Long before coins were invented, goods were traded by other means. The earliest civilizations of the Middle East and the Mediterranean were pastoral and their wealth was represented by flocks of sheep and goats and herds of cattle. Naturally, the earliest forms of money used by these peoples consisted of animals, meat and hides. Many of the words used in connection with money originated in this way. From the Latin word *pecus*, meaning "herd", we get the adjectives "pecuniary" and "peculiar" (that portion of the herd assigned to the cowherd for his own use). The word "talent", which now means an asset or natural gift, denoted a sum of money in Biblical times, but long before that the Greek word *talanton* meant a cowhide. When metal began

Below: A 15th-century illustration of Russian and Scandinavian traders bartering, from the Historia Gentibus Septentrionalibus *by Olaus Magnus.*

to be used as money, these tended to mimic the traditional currencies. Large pieces of copper were shaped roughly like cowhides to form money talents.

The modern word "bourse" is used to describe a place where merchants and businessmen meet to buy, sell and exchange goods. This is also derived from cattle, the ancient word *byrsa* meaning "cowhide". Even some of the terms still used to indicate the denominations of coins are derived from animal skins. Thus, the Croatian unit of currency, the kuna, takes its name from the pine marten, whose pelt was the basis of trade, while the rouble is named from the Russian word for a strip of leather.

Salt was an indispensable commodity, highly prized for its use in the preserving of meat, and therefore very desirable in barter. From the Latin word for salt (*sal*) we get the modern term "salary", and we still use the expression "worth his/her salt". Bars of

Forms of Barter Currency
Native Americans, shown here at a trading post in Manitoba, bartered animal skins for guns. From beaver pelts and buckskins came the "made beaver" tokens of the Hudson's Bay Company and the continuing use of the expression "buck" to mean a dollar.

salt were still being used as currency in Ethiopia until the early 20th century.

When we discuss the fineness of gold coins, we use the term "carat" (US "karat"), which is derived from *keration,* the Greek word for a carob bean. These beans, being of a uniform size, were used for weighing things. The Greeks also coined the words *drachma* ("handful") and *obol* (from *belos*, meaning "dart" or "spit"). The Anglo-Saxons had coins called sceats and in the Baltic states a skatiku was a small coin, but both came originally from a Teutonic word *scaz*, simply meaning "treasure" (like the modern German *Schatz*). The German mark got its name from the scratch on a gold ingot, while "shilling" comes from Old Norse *skilja*, "cut".

Above: Tea-junks are loaded at Tseen-Tang, depicted in this 1843 engraving of a typical Chinese scene.

Below: Tobacco ships dock on the James River, Virginia in the 18th century, from Bryant's History of America.

Union (1990) when money in the traditional sense had ceased to have any value. Candy and chewing gum circulated in Italy in the 1970s during shortages of small change. In 1811, Henri Christophe confiscated the Haitians' accumulated stock of gourds and made them the island's unit of currency, using them to buy coffee, with which he re-established foreign trade. To this day the unit is the *gourde*, alluding to this drastic measure.

Potato Stamp

During World War II the remote island of Tristan da Cunha was occupied by the Royal Navy. Previously the islanders had had no use for coined money, but for the convenience of the sailors the local barter commodity (potatoes) was integrated with sterling at the rate of 4 potatoes to the penny. This dual system was even expressed on the postage stamp, designed for local island mail.

almonds (India), rock salt (Rome and Ethiopia), dried fish (Scandinavia), tea bricks (China), cacao beans (Mexico), tobacco (North America, Central Africa, Indonesia and Melanesia) and potatoes (Tristan da Cunha). In Cambodia's recent history, Pol Pot's moneyless society banned all forms of currency except rice, which was traded or bartered in tins from 1975 to 1979.

Generally, barter eventually gives way to some form of money, but commodities have been pressed into service as money in times of emergency, in war or periods of economic upheaval. The best example of this is the cigarette, which was widely used as currency in Germany (1945–8) and the Soviet

Below: Soviet soldiers rolling cigarettes in World War II. Hard-to-find items such as tobacco and chocolate were often traded between soldiers and civilians.

PAYMENT IN GOODS

Barter is a system of trade whereby one commodity is exchanged for another, or for a service of some kind, without the use of money. It takes many forms, depending on whether it is carried out within a community or between different communities, and also according to the customs of the people and what goods they have to exchange. It probably arose informally but eventually led to indirect barter, where some objects were invested with a fixed value, whether traded or accumulated as status symbols or signs of wealth. Among the commodities that have acquired a monetary value at different times are

EARLY CURRENCIES

From actual goods, such as potatoes, salt and tea, which were useful in themselves, it was a logical progression to use objects as currencies which, while lacking a practical use, came to represent an actual value against which the worth of goods and services could be measured. While an assortment of cigarettes or chewing gum may be of little interest to a collector of coins, the same is not true of various forms of early money, some of which are collected as "curious currencies".

SHELL MONEY

From a very early date, people have been fascinated by sea shells. They are often attractive in appearance and not easy to come by, so it is hardly surprising that they should have acquired a monetary value. Strings of *Dentalium* shells were used as money by the native American tribes of the north-western Pacific coast, while armlets composed of *Tridacna* shells were traded in New Guinea. Strings of polished shell discs were used as money all over the Pacific, variously known as *diwara* (New Britain), *pele* (Bismarck Archipelago), *biruan* (Solomon Islands), *mauwai* (Bougainville), *rongo* (Malaita) or *sapis-api* (New Guinea).

Above and right: "Money cowries" featured in J.G. Wood's Natural History, *1854. The cowrie continues to be used as a motif on coins, a rather crude design appearing on this 17th-century lead bazaruk of the Dutch East India Company.*

Above: An Egyptian tomb painting showing workers recording and banking payments in grain.

By far the most popular forms of shell money were the cowrie species *Cypraea moneta* and *C. annulus,* which were threaded to make necklaces. According to Chinese tradition it was the so-called Yellow Emperor, Huang-di (2698 BC) who established this ancient monetary system, though written records point to the ancient Shang and Zhou dynasties as the chief developers of the cowrie unit. The Chinese ideogram *pei* means both a cowrie shell and money in general. Cowrie shells were found only on the most southerly shores of China, which enabled the emperor to control the supply and thus maintain their value. As the population

Below: Two ancient currencies that circulated until quite recently: a Japanese silver chogin of 1865–9 (right) and a gold bar from Vila Rica in Brazil (below), used during the regency of Don João of Portugal, 1799.

expanded, the number of genuine cowries was insufficient to meet demand, so the Chinese resorted to various substitutes in stone, bone, ivory or jade, carved to resemble a cowrie, and later bronze cast in the shape of the shell. Cowries were used as money in China until about 200 BC, but their use spread to India and Arabia and thence to Central and East Africa, and the cowrie survived as currency until about 1950. The shells even circulated as small change alongside metallic coins, tariffed at 60–400 to the franc in French West Africa (1900), 200 to the Indian rupee in Uganda (1895) and up to 1200 to the West African shilling in the Gold Coast (now Ghana). They even inspired coins in India and Africa – the kori of Kutch and the cauri of Guinea. The cedi, used in Ghana, is named from a local word meaning "small shell".

It is strange that such a sophisticated society as that of ancient Egypt seldom used coins. However, the Egyptians had a highly complex currency system based on units of weighed metals, called *deben* and *qedet*, which enabled the values of goods to be compared with each other. Taxes could be paid in barley or other grains. The royal granaries acted as banks; people deposited and withdrew the goods, and interest-bearing loans of grain were also made.

ORIGINS OF METAL MONEY

A metallic standard was adopted in Mesopotamia (modern Iraq) as long ago as 2500 BC. By 1500 BC metal rings and copper utensils of standard quality, size and weight were being used as money and were interchangeable with articles of gold and silver. Deals were recorded in terms of copper bowls and pitchers, while gold and silver (originally valued equally) were worth 40 times their weight in copper. By the 10th century BC a ratio of 1:13:3000

Curious Currency

Bracelets in the shape of horse-shoes, known by the Spanish name *manilla* ("manacle"), circulated as money on the Slave Coast of West Africa. Far from trying to stamp out this currency, British traders imported vast quantities made in Birmingham in an alloy of copper, lead and pewter, and the indigenous tribes came to prefer these to their own productions. A manilla was originally worth 30 cents but fell to 20 cents by 1900.

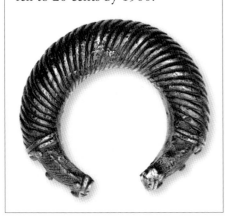

was established in the Middle East for gold, silver and copper respectively.

Such systems were by no means confined to the ancient world. Small bars and ingots stamped with the weight, fineness and issuing authority circulated as money in the Portuguese territories of Brazil and Mozambique in the 16th to 19th centuries, rather than the standard coinage of Portugal. Curiously shaped silver bars known as Tiger Tongues and bent rings sometimes called Banana Bars were used in Thailand and Vietnam, while copper bars known as Bonks circulated in the Dutch East Indies. These areas had coinage, introduced from India in the 7th and 8th centuries, but by the 11th century it had disappeared and been replaced by silver ingots, of which these are just a few varieties.

It can be hard to understand why certain kinds of currency should sometimes have been preferred to coins. In some cases, as in colonial Brazil, the local currency was employed of necessity because of poor communications with the mother country. In another example, playing cards marked with values were used in 17th-century Canada instead of French coins. In South-east Asia, however, the curiously shaped pieces of silver were used, rather than flat discs, merely because that was the traditional style. For the same reasons, many of the petty kingdoms and states in India preferred copper and silver bars. It was traditional, and people had confidence in money of that kind, whereas coins in the Western sense were unfamiliar and not trusted.

During the Shogunate of the 17th to 19th centuries, Japan had the most elaborate metallic system of all, involving bars of copper (kwan-ei) and silver (chogin), rectangular gold ingots (ichibu and nibu kin) and large elliptical gold plates known as oban and koban. These had a ribbed surface on which symbols and inscriptions were countermarked. The oban were additionally inscribed with their weight and the mint-master's signature in black ink, using traditional brush techniques.

Above: A beautiful example of a gold koban of pre-Meiji Japan, with large piercing on the reverse.

NON-METALLIC SUBSTITUTES

Pieces of leather have served as money at various times in many parts of the world. As recently as 1923–4, during the German hyperinflation, pieces of shoe leather were stamped with values in millions of marks, and circular pieces of leather embossed with coin images were used in Austria. Pottery and porcelain tokens were used in China and Thailand in the mid-19th century, while in 1945 Japan resorted to terracotta coins of 1, 2 and 5 sen to combat wartime inflation. In the 19th and early 20th centuries the Chinese exchanged bamboo sticks stamped with brands to denote transactions from 100 cash upwards. Apart from a series of commemorative coins in 1977, the only currencies to circulate in the Cocos (Keeling) Islands are tokens of porcelain or plastic, which are used on the coconut plantations.

Below: Tokens exchanged on colonial plantations were often given actual currency values. This brass 1 dollar token is from the Dutch East Indies.

CHINESE COINAGE

The development of the earliest coinage was roughly simultaneous in China and Asia Minor. The first Chinese "coins" were small pieces of bronze, cast and fashioned into representations of the useful agricultural implements used in barter, such as spades and bill-hooks. The small knives, spades, keys and other domestic articles, symbols of the earlier barter system, were invested with a notional value and had no utilitarian purpose. But they represented a real value and could be exchanged for goods or services accordingly.

The knives were about 15cm/6in long and bore the value and the name of the issuing authority. The bu currency, a modified form of the bronze spades, circulated widely in the 5th and 4th centuries BC, and their image has even been reproduced on Chinese coins in modern times.

THE ARRIVAL OF CASH
By the 4th century BC, bronze circular discs with a hole in the centre were in circulation. Over several generations

Right: Bronze knife money used during the Warring States period.

Below: A cast imitation cowrie (with a central hole), and an example of the round-hooked "spade" money.

The Silver Yuan

Spanish, Mexican, British and American trade dollars circulated extensively in China and filled the need for coins of higher denominations, so it was not until the late 19th century that China began minting silver coins of its own. The yuan (dollar) was introduced in 1889 at par with the Mexican peso. It circulated alongside the foreign silver, but in order to provide pieces of the same weight and fineness as the other trade dollars already in circulation the Chinese had to produce coins of odd values, based on the traditional Chinese weight and value system of mace and candareens. A handsome piece, nicknamed the Sichuan rupee and issued in Tibet, appeared in the closing years of the century and was the only coin actually to portray the Manchu emperor.

Above: Pattern silver dollar produced by the central Tianjin mint in 1911.

Above: Silver dragon and phoenix dollar of the Chinese Republic, 1923.

these pieces evolved into the regular banliang (half-ounce) coins minted by the Emperor Shi Huang-di, founder of the Qin dynasty, in 221 BC and known as cash. In 118 BC the banliang were replaced by wuzhu (5 grain) coins by the Han emperor Wudi. These were used all over China, even after the empire was split into a number of smaller states in AD 220. In 621, after the empire was reunified, the Tang emperor Gaozu replaced the wuzhu with a new design with four, rather than two, characters. This style remained in use until 1911. Thus, the Chinese cash, with its distinctive square hole and inscriptions in ideograms, was in circulation for over two millennia. The four Chinese characters that appear on the traditional cash signify "current money of", followed by the

Right: An iron cash coin bearing Chinese and Manchu legends, produced by the Qing dynasty.

Above: A Chinese bazaar. Despite attempts by various governors to revive larger currencies, the portable copper cash coin remained part of everyday trade for more than 2000 years.

symbol of the appropriate reign. The currency name is not related to the English word for ready money (which comes from the French *caisse* and Italian *cassa,* meaning "money box"). Rather, it appears in slightly different forms in many Oriental languages, from the Sanskrit *karsa* and Persian *karsha* ("weight") via Tamil *kacu* and Portuguese *caixa*, denoting a small copper coin.

Below: Copper cash obverses from the reigns of Emperors Hongxian (1915) and Guangxu (1905).

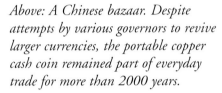

Above: Reinstated bu (bronze knife and key) money of Wang Mang.

Bu money was briefly revived by the usurper Wang Mang (AD 7–23), but decimalized. Copper cash spread to Korea in the 3rd century BC and Japan (AD 708). Cash continued as the money of China itself and was not superseded until the overthrow of the Qing dynasty and the proclamation of the republic in 1911. Even then, Western-style bronze coins, introduced in 1912 and featuring the crossed flags of the new regime, continued to be denominated in cash, and it is believed that traditional copper cash continued to circulate in rural areas until 1925.

THE ARRIVAL OF CASH

Although various denominations of cash existed, the basic cash unit had a very small value, and the Chinese got into the habit of creating larger values by stringing them together into the shape of a sword. By the time of the Tang dynasty, between AD 650 and 800, merchants found the transportation of huge wagonloads of cash around the country not only cumbersome but insecure, at the mercy of bandits, so they invented *fei-ch'ien* (literally "flying money"), consisting of paper drafts negotiable in bronze currency. These drafts were not authorized paper money in the modern sense but undoubtedly paved the way for the bank notes introduced much later, that serve the world for higher amounts of money.

Above: A Chinese watercolour depicting a moneylender weighing out coins under the Qing dynasty.

Below: The Chinese were pioneers of the use of paper money. This 1000 cash note was issued in 1854, under the Qing dynasty. The rectangular red stamp is the seal of the Fukien Yung Feng Official Bureau.

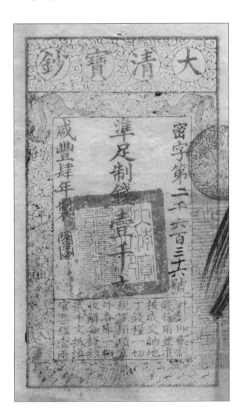

GREEK COINAGE

Copper was worked in Cyprus from at least 3000 BC (indeed, the name of the island is derived from the Greek word for the metal) and by the middle Bronze Age it was being cast into bullion bars, called talents. An ancient Greek talent of bronze (an alloy of copper and tin) weighed about 60lb/127kg. The talent used at the time of Homer, in the 9th century BC, was said to be made of gold, while the talent of Attica, the district surrounding Athens, was of silver, divided into 60 units known as *minae*, worth 100 drachmae each. These units of weight were widely used for high-value transactions in the ancient world.

LEAVING A MARK
Gold was regarded as being worth 13 pieces of silver of equivalent weight, or 3000 pieces of copper. An alloy of gold and silver called electrum, often referred to as pale gold or white gold,

Below: Leaden coin weights used in ancient Greece. The inscriptions on the bottom two suggest that they are equivalent to 8 and 2 drachmae.

Above: Electrum coinage of the Lydian kings with an open-mouthed lion on the obverse (top). The Turtles of Aegina (bottom) circulated widely through the Greek Empire and beyond. The reverse of this stater from 700–500 BC bears an interesting incuse (recessed) punch mark.

was popular in the earliest period. For centuries merchants were accustomed to weigh out lumps of metal at every transaction, but gradually a more convenient system was devised. A rich merchant, or a prince on whose land the metal was mined, would cast it into lumps of uniform size and weight and guarantee the weight of these lumps by applying his personal mark to them. At first this stamp consisted of an irregular mark, made by striking the metal with a broken nail. The jagged edge of the nail left an individual mark that served to identify the person who issued the metal. Sometimes these lumps had several marks struck on them in the form of a pattern. As a rule, the marks appeared on one side only, though the reverse might have a pattern of lines, where the anvil had dug into the metal during striking.

COINS IN A MODERN SENSE
According to the Greek historian Herodotus, the Lydians were the first people to use gold and silver coins. From the evidence of coin hoards and archaeological research it is now believed that the earliest coins of Lydia were produced in the late 7th century BC. By 630 BC the crude nail mark had developed into a proper design, the lion's head emblem of the Mermnad

dynasty of Lydia, of which King Croesus – whose wealth was proverbial in the ancient world – was the fifth and last ruler. This emblem was applied to the obverse, or "heads" side, by placing the lump of metal (called a blank or flan) on an anvil whose top had been engraved with the design. The flan had been heated until it was very soft, and striking it with a hammer impressed the image into the surface of the metal. At first the hammer had no mark on its surface, and the earliest coins were uniface (one-sided), but gradually it became customary to include a simple geometric design that bit into the reverse, or "tails" side, of the coin, giving an "incuse" reverse (a simple hammered design). The authority that these simple designs afforded came to be regarded as a guarantee of their value. The value was still linked to the

Below: Ancient Greek coins were highly innovative. This Corinthian stater (top) has a winged Pegasus with a concave reverse showing a helmeted Athena. The coin of Lucania (now Italy) bears a wheat ear with a simple incuse reverse (middle), while the coin of Miletus, a coastal colony in Asia Minor, bears interesting geometric designs (bottom).

The Ornate Shield of Macedon

Philip of Macedon welded the Greeks into a nation and his son Alexander the Great created an empire in the 4th century BC. After his death, the empire was divided and Macedon passed to his general, Antigonus. His descendant, Antigonus Gonatas (277–239 BC), struck this shield-shaped coin bearing the head of Pan. The reverse shows Athena Alkis holding a shield and thunderbolt. These ornate coins survived until Macedon was absorbed by the Roman Empire in the 2nd century BC.

This pattern survived until the early Christian era, though latterly the coins were confined to bronze and permitted by the Romans only for local circulation. The designs were faithfully reproduced in the coinage of modern Greece and survive to this day on the national reverses of the euro coinage.

By the 4th century BC coinage was in general use throughout the Greek world, including colonies as far afield as Syracuse (Sicily) and Marseilles. Silver predominated and coins ranged in size from the tiny hemi-obol to the massive decadrachm (10 drachmae). Portraiture was generally confined to gods and heroes, but after the death of Alexander his profile appeared on coins of the Hellenistic kingdoms created by his generals, and later they used their own portraits.

Above: One of many posthumous coins struck for Alexander the Great, after his death in 323 BC.

Below: The coinage of Alexander the Great, depicted in battle on this ceramic vase, greatly influenced ancient and medieval coins in Europe and Asia.

weight and precious metal content, but it was no longer necessary to weigh each piece at every transaction.

THE SPREAD OF COINS

The first electrum coins were found in the river bed of the Pactolus in Asia Minor and may have been struck under the authority of King Ardys of Lydia,

Below: Electrum and silver trihemibols of Phocaea (Ionia), in western Anatolia.

ancestor of Croesus. From there they spread to other parts of western Asia Minor, being adopted by the Greek coastal towns of Abydus, Chios, Miletus and Phocaea. These early coins needed no inscriptions, as they circulated only within their own territories, but their motifs were clues to their identity, such as the sphinx of Chios and the man-bull of Miletus. One of the earliest Greek coins showed the civic emblem of a stag and was inscribed "I am the sign of Phanes". It is still the subject of debate as to whether Phanes was a place or a person.

Coin production spread from Asia Minor to mainland Greece in the 6th century. Aegina led the way with its silver "Turtles", whose reverse had a geometric incuse pattern not unlike a Union Jack. Nearby Corinth followed with drachmae showing the winged horse Pegasus. Athens possessed silver mines that enabled it to strike a vast quantity of coins, which were soon accepted all over the Greek world. The earliest featured a range of motifs, but in 546 BC Pisistratus instituted the coins bearing a helmeted profile of Athena on the obverse and an owl, symbol of wisdom, on the reverse.

ROMAN COINAGE

Our connection with the Roman world can be detected in many of our units of currency and weight. The Latin word *pondus*, for example, has given us such words as "ponder" (to weigh up), "ponderous" (heavy) and "pound", used both as a weight (lb) and a unit of currency (£). The abbreviations for the pound in weight and money both came from another Latin word – *libra*, meaning a pound. This is preserved in many European currencies, as *lira* (Italy, Israel and Turkey) or *livre* (France).

Although an imperial mint to supply silver and gold coins was not established in Rome until 269 BC, the Romans had been striking bronze coins locally for several decades prior to this. These bronze currencies began with the aes rude, whose name refers to the crudeness of unmarked lumps of metal, which had to be weighed out at each transaction. Gradually, the lumps were replaced by bars or ingots of a uniform shape and weight. They were known as aes signatum ("signed bronze") because they bore the stamp of the issuing authority on both sides. Significantly,

Below: The Romans were highly skilled in financial dealings. This relief from a Gallo-Roman mausoleum shows a tax collector at work.

Above: Roman aes grave coins, denominated as triens and sextans.

one of these was a bull, alluding to the importance of cattle as a form of barter currency in earlier times.

After aes signatum came aes grave ("heavy bronze"). These pieces were roughly circular and fairly flat – like coins, but very much heavier. The basic unit was the as, weighing a pound (*libra*) and bearing the Roman numeral I. Half of this was the semis, indicated by the letter S. A third of an as was the triens, which, being worth four Roman ounces, bore four little pellets to indicate its weight and value. Smaller units were the quadrans ("fourth"), sextans ("sixth") and the uncia ("ounce", indicated by one pellet).

This heavy bronze coinage coincided with the inception of the Roman Mint, which issued a series of silver coins, influenced by the penchant for figures of deities and their familiars in Greek coin design. The series consisted of didrachms (2 drachmae) and their subdivisions of litra, half-litra and silver as. Ten asses of silver or bronze were worth a silver didrachm. The silver coins were inscribed "Roma" or "Romano".

At this point, bronze coins began to fall out of favour. Their weight and consequent value were progressively reduced, until the bronze as eventually weighed no more than the original uncia coin.

GOLD AND SILVER COINS

The Romans preferred silver coins because the metal was abundant, and could be made into a hard-wearing alloy by adding a little copper. Gold was regarded primarily as a medium for jewellery; it was very rarely used for coins. Gold staters were struck in 216 BC during a shortage of silver as a result of the wars against Carthage. (A small silver coin, equivalent to a drachma but known as a victoriate, was struck to celebrate the defeat of Carthage.)

Its victories in the Punic Wars made Rome the most powerful state in the western Mediterranean. Its prosperity led to the adoption of a new currency in 211 BC, based on the silver denarius – the forerunner of the deniers and dinars used by many European and Asiatic countries (and preserved in Britain until 1971 in the symbol "d" to denote the penny). The denarius of 10 asses was divided into the quinarius (5 asses) and the sestertius (2½ asses). A board of moneyers, consisting of three officials elected annually, was created, and their names, initials or family emblems began to appear on the coins.

PORTRAITURE AND ALLEGORY

From the 2nd century BC, Roman coins became more elaborate in their design. The most popular images were Roma and Bellona on the obverse and the heavenly twins, Castor and Pollux, on the reverse. From 146 BC, when the Romans finally destroyed the city of Carthage, Rome expanded rapidly, acquiring territory in North Africa, Gaul (France) and Iberia (Spain), suppressing the Greek colonies in southern Italy and advancing into the Balkans. Coins of this period featured Victory, Mars and Jupiter on the obverse, with elaborate designs illustrating characters and events in classical mythology.

In 141 BC the currency was revalued on the basis of the denarius of 16 asses. Scholars have many theories concerning the motive for this, the general view

Above: The coins of Antoninus Pius featured a seated Britannia (right).

Above: Some imperial gold coins circulated as far as India, like this holed gold aureus of Caracalla (top). A solidus of Valens appears below.

Coins in Memoriam

The Emperor Augustus struck coins in memory of his predecessor Julius Caesar, while the coin shown here was struck by Tiberius in memory of Augustus.

now being that silver had become much more plentiful, leading to a decrease in the value of the as. The increase from 10 to 16 asses in the denarius seems to have been a balancing adjustment.

Coins became more varied in design as the moneyers rivalled each other in depicting emblems and events alluding to their illustrious ancestors. By the first century BC, portraits of ancestors were appearing, while Rome was splitting into political factions under such men as Marius, Sulla, Pompey and Julius Caesar. Caesar struck coins in Gaul that included the numerals LII (52, his age) – one of the earliest attempts at putting a date on a coin. After 49 BC, when he became master of Rome, his coins took on a more personal character, with

lengthy inscriptions referring to his various public offices. The last coins under Julius Caesar's authority actually bore his portrait.

THE ROMAN EMPIRE

From Caesar's assassination in 44 BC until the battle of Actium in 31 BC, a period of civil wars was marked by coins struck on behalf of Brutus, Cassius, the sons of Pompey, the triumvirate of Mark Antony, Lepidus and Octavian, and finally for Octavian himself, having assumed the title of Augustus and set about transforming Rome into an empire. In 27 BC he accepted the title of emperor and instituted a new coinage based on the gold aureus, worth 25 silver denarii. Smaller coins included the brass sestertius and the dupondius (2 asses). Although the weights and sizes of these coins varied, the denominations remained in use for most of the Roman Imperial period.

Imperial coins were prolific and served as propaganda for the emperor, extolling his virtues and achievements and often portraying his wife and family as well as himself. They were generally well produced, with realistic portraits, and elaborate allegorical compositions on the reverse. The seated figure of Britannia shown on British coins since 1672 was actually modelled on the Britannia featured on coins of

Antoninus Pius (138–61), in whose reign the Antonine Wall across the isthmus of the Forth and Clyde was built.

The double denarius, or antoninianus, was introduced in AD 214 under Caracalla. By that time inflation had caused the demise of the denarius and thereafter the antoninianus was the basic unit of currency. Although nominally silver, it was progressively debased and eventually was no more than a copper coin with a thin silver wash, which soon wore off. New coins were the follis (AD 294) and the gold solidus (309), ancestor of such European coins as the soldo, sol and sou, and the source of the "s" denoting the shilling in pre-decimal British currency.

The nummus, introduced by Diocletian between AD 295 and 310, played a major part in the development of Byzantine coinage. During the 4th century there were two new silver coins, the miliarense and the siliqua, and finally the tremissis, a gold piece worth a third of a solidus.

Below: The expanding Roman empire struck denarii following acquisitions in France (Gallic shield on coin, top) and the Balkans (head of Victory, bottom).

Below: Seminal coins issued by the Roman Republic to mark the assassination of Julius Caesar (top) and the suicide of Mark Antony (bottom).

BYZANTINE COINAGE

In AD 364, Valentinian divided the Roman Empire into eastern and western provinces, assigning the Eastern Empire to his brother Valens. From that time there were two Roman Empires, based in the cities of Rome and Byzantium (Constantinople) respectively. The Western Empire came to an end in 476, when the last emperor, Romulus Augustulus, was defeated by the Ostrogoths. Their ruler, Theodoric, minted coins with his portrait on one side and a figure of Rome on the other, with the caption "Invicta Roma" ("Unconquered Rome"), but these coins were very crude by comparison with the classical issues, and they formed an ironic tailpiece to seven centuries of Roman coinage.

THE IMPERIAL TRADITION

In the east, the Roman Empire survived a further thousand years, until the capture of Constantinople by the Turks in 1453. At the height of its

Above: Constantine V (left) and a portrait of Christ (middle) on a coin that shows the joint rulers, Basil II and Constantine VIII on the reverse (right).

Below: Allegorical designs on coins of Anastasius and John II portray the emperors flanked by Victory.

Above: Crusaders at the walls of Constantinople in 1204, depicted in De la Conquête de Constantinople *by Geoffroi de Villehardouin.*

power, the Byzantine Empire extended over the eastern Mediterranean, including even parts of Italy. It retained the ancient Roman provinces in the Balkans and controlled Asia Minor, Syria and Palestine.

Byzantium became the repository of Roman technology, science and the accumulated wisdom of the classical world, and it was the flight of scholars and scientists from Turkish rule after the conquest that triggered off the Renaissance (the rebirth of learning) in the West. Just as the Byzantine Empire kept alight the lamp of learning and civilization in early medieval times, so did it continue the traditions of Greece and Rome in its coins. A new feature, however, was the portrayal of the emperor full-face instead of in profile.

Since the time of the Emperor Constantine (who believed that the victory that gave him the throne had been aided by the one God of the Christians), Christianity had been the official religion of the empire, and from its foundation in 324 his capital at Constantinople, on the site of the ancient Byzantium, had been a Christian city. This religious devotion found expression on the coins of the Byzantine Empire. The figure of Jesus Christ appears on the obverse of Byzantine coins from about 450, followed by the Virgin Mary. From the 9th century onward many saints of the Orthodox Church – Theodore, George, Michael and John among others – were portrayed on the reverses. Christian symbolism replaced the pagan allegory of the Roman Empire.

CHANGING STYLES

As time went by, Greek replaced Latin in the inscriptions on these coins, and it is interesting to note how the Greek letters gradually took over from their Roman counterparts. Inevitably the standards of design and production slipped over the centuries, although

---

Saucer-shaped Coins

Coins were produced on a flat disc flan until the reign of Constantine IX (1042–55), when a curious concave shape was adopted for all denominations except the smallest bronze pieces. These are known to collectors as *nummi scyphati* (literally "boat-shaped coins"). In succeeding reigns the flan became thinner and slightly cup-shaped, but the strange shape endured until the Latin conquest of 1204.

Byzantine coinage continued to be far superior to that produced anywhere else in the medieval world. Unlike their Roman predecessors, Byzantine coins were relatively neglected by collectors, who regarded their designs as stereotyped and rather monotonous, but recently collectors have developed a keen interest, discovering the subtle developments in design as well as the light they shed on a period of European history that is not well documented in written records. Not surprisingly, coins that not so long ago were comparatively cheap have soared in value.

Although it lasted a millennium, the Byzantine Empire was not a static entity but expanded and contracted, assailed by foreign invasion and torn by civil wars, and these highs and lows of its history are reflected in the coinage. Constantinople was besieged by the Arabs in 674 and the Bulgars in 923. In 1204, during the Fourth Crusade, it fell to these holy warriors and was under Latin (that is, Western European) rule from then until 1261.

The Byzantines minted coins in bronze, silver and gold, although their silver coins are comparatively scarce and usually debased by a high copper

Below: Emperor Justinian I and his wife Theodora, both of whom featured on Byzantine coins.

Above: Lengthy Graeco-Roman inscriptions on post-Justinian coins.

Below: Byzantine coin weights: a 2 solidi square weight (left), a nomisma square weight (right) and a ⅓ nomisma circular weight (bottom).

content. Justinian I was the first emperor to add a date to his coins, in the form of the year from the beginning of his reign, 526. As well as the increasingly bewildering mixture of Roman and Greek lettering, often reducing inscriptions to little more than an apparent jumble of initials, the collector has to contend with the use of letters to denote numerals in dates and denominations. New titles, such as "Autokrator" (Emperor) and "Basileus Romaion" (King of the Romans) in Greek capitals vie with the cryptic "MP QV" (*Meter Theou* or Mother of God) and "IC" or "XC" (Jesus Christ).

DENOMINATIONS

The currency was originally based on the gold solidus and its subdivisions, down to the tiny sixth, which was the equivalent of two silver hexagrams. Gradually, the Byzantines adopted a new name for the solidus, calling it

a nomisma. In the reign of Nicephorus II a lighter coin than the solidus was adopted, known as a tetarteron, on par with the Arab dinar. In the time of Michael IV (1034–41) the nomisma underwent progressive debasement. Its gold content had dropped to about 26 per cent by the time Alexius I reformed the coinage in 1092 and introduced the hyperper, nominally of pure gold but averaging 21 carat fineness.

The basic silver coin was originally the miliaresion. This word literally means a thousandth part – but of what remains a mystery, as it was tariffed at 12 to the solidus. It was replaced in the reign of Heraclius (610–41) by a crude coin of the same value known as a hexagram. By the 9th century the miliaresion was much thinner and lighter and seems to have been worth half a hexagram. Silver coinage did not recover until the end of the 13th century and was then modelled on contemporary Venetian types, reflecting Venice's control of Byzantine trade.

Copper coins were based on the follis of 40 nummia, the number being represented by a large M. The half (20 nummia) was indicated by the letter K and the quarter by the letter I. Billon (an alloy of copper with a small amount of silver) was used for the trachy, tariffed at 48 to the hyperper.

Above: The basic silver coin of the Byzantine Empire: the miliaresion.

Below: The follis of 40 nummia, a large and cumbersome coin, widely used as small change.

OTHER ANCIENT EUROPEAN COINAGE

Parallel with the main developments of coinage in the great civilizations of the Greek, Roman and Byzantine worlds were the attempts by the peoples beyond the fringes of the civilized world to emulate them. The groups discussed here are the ones of major interest to coin collectors. There were many others that are either obscure, or that produced relatively little coinage, or were content to copy the coins of their more powerful neighbours.

CELTIC COINAGE
The Celtic peoples settled the valley of the Danube and occupied the area now forming the countries of Switzerland, France, Spain, Germany, Belgium and the Netherlands. They migrated to the British Isles around 600 BC and their cultural legacy, especially in Ireland, the Scottish Highlands, Cumbria, Wales and Cornwall, remains strong to this day. Paradoxically, the Celtic fringes of the British Isles did not produce distinctive coinage, but elsewhere, including the southerly and eastern areas of what eventually formed Roman Britain, distinctive Celtic coins developed in the late pre-Christian era.

The Danubian Celts imitated the gold and silver coins with which they were most familiar, the silver

Below: Celtic coins of France and Spain include this Iberian coin of Osca with a horseman (top) and a Gallo-Belgic stater with a large flan depicting Apollo.

Above: Celtic designs: a vine leaf stater of Verica (top), the Phoenician goddess Tanit on a coin of the Danubian Celts (middle) and a stater of the Iceni with a horse and wheel (bottom).

tetradrachms and gold staters of the Alexandrine Empire and its Hellenistic successors, but because they were illiterate they blundered the inscriptions or abandoned them altogether. At the same time, the profiles of Philip of Macedon and Alexander the Great were reduced to caricature and then all but vanished, only curls and headbands surviving. Similarly, the horseman on the reverse was reduced to a stylized, abstract shape.

Not so long ago, Celtic coinage was dismissed as barbaric because of this abstraction of classical patterns, but now scholars and collectors are discovering the extraordinary vitality of Celtic art and the religious symbolism of the human heads and even the curvilinear motifs, which are startlingly avant-garde in appearance. British Celts latterly included brief inscriptions that identify the rulers of the Atrebates, Durotriges, Catuvellauni, Iceni, Trinovantes and others in the period immediately before the Roman conquest in AD 43.

THE FALL OF ROME
The minting of coins was one of the technologies lost in the collapse of the Roman Empire. Crude copies of Roman coins were produced by the Ostrogoths, Germanic people who

---

Anglo-Saxon Portraiture
The vast majority of early Anglo-Saxon coins had some sort of cross on the reverse. Portraits were seldom attempted and were extremely crude and virtually unrecognizable as such. Unique gold coins of Offa (c. 780) and Archbishop Wigmund of York (837–54) have portraits in the Roman or Byzantine style, but these were quite exceptional. It was not until 973 that a royal effigy became standard: the image was composed of tiny punch marks, such as on this penny of Edward the Martyr of 975.

---

eventually ruled the Romans, from the end of the 5th century. Theodoric the Great not only paid homage to the memory of Imperial Rome but slavishly copied the gold coins of his Byzantine contemporary Anastasius, even going so far as to copy his titles and inscriptions. His successors, Athalaric and Theodahad, substituted

Below: A Celtic punch-marked coin of the Durotriges (top) and an Ostrogoth imitation of a Roman 40 nummia.

Above: Coins of early medieval France include this tremissis struck by the Visigoths in the name of Severus (top) and 12th-century billon deniers of Burgundy (bottom).

Above and right: The Vikings established extensive trade links. Viking pennies, such as these of Daegmund and Arus, have been found throughout Europe.

their own portraits. For a time the Byzantine rulers recovered the Balkans and Italy from the Goths and struck coins at Rome and Ravenna in the 8th and 9th centuries.

Elsewhere in the early medieval world, coins based on Roman models were struck by the Vandals in North Africa, denominated in both Roman siliquae and denarii, the Suevians in Spain, the Lombards in Italy, the Burgundians in northern France, the Visigoths in the south of that country, and the Anglo-Saxons in England.

In the majority of cases these coins followed Roman precedents, incorporating crude portraits of local rulers and a wide variety of local inscriptions. Whereas coin production was centralized at the Roman Mint, the rulers of the early medieval European kingdoms dispersed the process and granted the right to strike coins to many towns, and even to monasteries. In the Merovingian kingdom of the 6th and 7th centuries, for example, there existed more than 800 mints. The Merovingians, who ruled over parts of present-day France and Germany, introduced a new coin, the silver saiga, based on the Roman denarius. The legacy of this coin was far-reaching: it led to the denier or penny, introduced by Pepin the Short in 755.

VIKING AND ANGLO-SAXON COINAGE

The money that was used in Britain between the withdrawal of the Roman legions, early in the 5th century, and the advent of William the Conqueror, in 1066, is generally described as Anglo-Saxon, although distinctive types were adopted in the seven main kingdoms (Northumbria, Mercia, Kent, East Anglia, Essex, Sussex and Wessex), which emerged as a united England in 959 under Eadgar and adopted the silver penny as the standard unit of currency in 973.

The earliest coins were known as sceats or sceattas (derived from the Old English word meaning "wealth"), and were small pieces of base silver and latterly copper with a uniquely eclectic mixture of symbolism derived from Roman, Byzantine, Teutonic and Celtic coins. Offa of Mercia (757–96) introduced the silver penny, adapted from the Carolingian denier (denarius) with a crude effigy on the obverse and a cross on the reverse. The thrymsa was a small gold coin derived from the tremissis (or third solidus), which was struck between 575 and about 775.

The Vikings traded as widely as they raided and made use of the coinage of other countries, notably England, whose silver penny became the model for the earliest distinctive coins in Denmark, Norway and Sweden. Hedeby in Denmark and Birka in Sweden, the major trading centres of Scandinavia, produced vast quantities of silver pennies with distinctive motifs and runic inscriptions. English sterlings were also extensively copied, not only in the Danelaw (that part of England under Danish rule from the late 9th century), but also in the Norse kingdoms in Ireland and the Isle of Man.

Below: Anglo-Saxon silver pennies issued in Mercia (top) and by the authority of King Eadgar (bottom).

MEDIEVAL EUROPEAN COINAGE

With the collapse of the Roman Empire in Western Europe, social structures became more localized and the coinage system was fragmented. Under the Carolingian rulers, who rose to power as kings of the Franks in the 8th century, a new standardized system was imposed. The gold coins in the realm were demonetized, and in 752 Pepin the Short issued a new silver coin, the silver denier (based on the Roman denarius), which became the basic unit of currency.

BIRTH OF THE SILVER PENNY

The denier was a practical coin for the early Middle Ages, when barter was still prevalent and most people required coins only as a means of converting a small agricultural surplus into cash, and it remained the standard unit for nearly

Below: An enormous salut d'or of Henry VI, with the arms of England and France, to which Henry laid claim, and a depiction of the annunciation.

six centuries. In 793, Charlemagne increased the weight of the denier by a third, and as his empire grew, so his coinage was imitated in the denar of the Balkans (hence the dinar of Serbia to this day), the denaro of Italy and the dinero of Spain. It also provided the model for the penny, which travelled from 9th-century England to Scandinavia and northern Germany, giving rise to the pfennig or pfenning in the German states, the fenigow in Poland and the penni in Finland.

By the 11th century the use of the denier was more or less confined to France, where it was struck at many mints – royal, baronial and ecclesiastical. The inconvenience of having no larger coins led to the introduction by Louis IX (1226–70) of the gros (from the French for "large"), which spread across Europe in many different forms – grote, groat, groschen, groszy, grush and even the Turkish kurus.

Below: A 13th-century silver gros tournois of Philip III of France (top), and papal testones of Pius IV (middle), with St Peter enthoned, and Sixtus V (bottom), with St Peter standing.

Above: Workers of the 15th century being paid by the Commune of Siena, in a painting by Pietro di Sano.

Below: A cavallino d'oro of Sicily (top) and a 16th-century zecchino of Venice.

ITALIAN AND GERMAN COINS

After the collapse of the Roman Empire, Italy disintegrated into a multitude of petty principalities and city states. It was the crossroads of civilization and came under the influence of Romans, Byzantines, Goths, Franks and Arabs, reflected in complex coinage of many different types. Pope Adrian I (772–95) minted the first papal coins, which continue to this day.

By the 12th century the city states of Italy were in the forefront of the commercial revolution, and their prosperity was reflected in the size and quality of their coins, as well as the extent to which they were coveted and

Above: A Venetian silver ducato, showing the Doge kneeling before St Mark, and the winged lion.

Above (from top): Gold guldens of medieval Hungary and Germany; Crusader coins range from this copper type of Tancred of Antioch to this ornate silver gros of Bohemond VI.

because they were fragile and easily damaged, but it meant that a small amount of silver went a long way and enabled much larger coins to be struck.

ARABIC INFLUENCES

Gold coins were reintroduced in Western Europe from the 13th century, as the general level of prosperity recovered after the Early Medieval period. This was first evident in southern Italy, where the gold tari and copper follari, originally modelled on the Byzantine system, were inscribed in a mixture of Latin and Arabic. Byzantium was also the inspiration for the silver ducat, so-called because it was first struck in the Duchy (*ducatus*) of Apulia.

From the end of the first millennium the nation-states of Europe gradually emerged, but the process of centralizing coin production and introducing uniformity went on for several centuries. As well as the numerous coins issued by nobles in their own fiefdoms, Crusader coins emanating from the Latin kingdoms briefly flourished in various parts of the Balkans, Asia Minor, Syria and Palestine in the 12th and 13th centuries. Interestingly, it was in the Crusader kingdoms that the pattern of French feudal coinage was most closely followed, although while imitating the deniers of the West they were often influenced by the sizes, weights, specifications and designs of their Islamic contemporaries.

Below: A bilingual tram of Armenia with an inscription citing the Seljuqs of Rum (top) and imitation dirhams of the 13th century (bottom).

Bracteates

Coins so thin that they can be struck on only one side are known as bracteates, derived from *bractea*, the medieval Latin word for gold or silver leaf. Coins so described range from the "shadow" coins interred with the dead in ancient Greece to those used in Viking jewellery. The term is also used for the extremely thin silver coins popular in the German states in the 12th to 14th centuries, with emblems struck on one side showing through to the reverse. Popularly known as *Hohlpfennige* (hollow pennies), they circulated alongside more orthodox coins and may have served purely as local small change.

copied elsewhere. Venice, the greatest trading city of this period, introduced the zecchino or sequin, while its rival Florence produced a large silver coin in 1189 depicting a lily (the flower from which it derived its name). The coin, called a fiorino or florin, eventually passed into the currency of many countries, surviving until 2002 in the Netherlands (where the written symbol for a gulden was "fl"). From Genoa in the mid-13th century came the genovino, one of the first great trade gold coins. Worth 20 solidi or 240 denari, it helped to bolster the Roman £sd system, previously confined to money of account rather than actual currency.

In Germany the Franks were at first content to imitate the Romans and Byzantines. In the 14th century, Louis of Bavaria introduced the grossus, modelled on the French gros, and many of the German states adopted thin silver bracteates. It is hard to understand why these were so popular,

MIDDLE EASTERN COINAGE

The inhabitants of Arabia had no coins of their own and were content to use Sassanian drachmae of Persia and the copper folles of Byzantium. Even after they began their dramatic expansion throughout the Middle East, borrowed coinage remained the norm, but in the mid-7th century Caliph Abd al-Malik introduced coinage based on the gold dinar (denarius aureus), the silver dirham (drachma) and the bronze fils (follis). At first the caliph was content to use Byzantine gold solidi, but because they bore the image of Christ he decided to issue his own gold coins with non-figurative motifs, hence the dinar, whose appearance coincided with the rise of iconoclasm in Islam.

DYNASTIC COINS

By the mid-7th century the great empires of Persia and Byzantium had fought each other to a standstill. In the resulting power vacuum the religious zeal of the Arabs gave their aggressive expansion a powerful incentive and explains why they were able to overrun the Middle East so rapidly. Umar, the Commander of the Faithful, established Basra in Mesopotamia and Fustat in Egypt as major centres from which the Arabs spread across the Middle East and North Africa, and thence into Central Asia and the Iberian Peninsula.

Below: An Abd al-Malik dinar of AH 78 (top) and a dirham of AH 81.

Above: More than a thousand years of Arab influence on Spanish coin production can be seen in this 18th-century dirham of Marrakesh struck at Madrid (top) and in this Arab-Byzantine dirham circulated in 8th-century Spain (bottom).

First and foremost of the Arab dynasties were the Umayyads. At the height of their power they ruled over a vast territory from Seville to Bokhara, but they were overthrown in 750. From their chief mint at Wasit they produced the first of the silver dirhams with Koranic inscriptions on both sides, establishing a pattern that lasted for centuries, imitated by their successors, the Abbasids, and later rival dynasties such as the Fatimids of Egypt and the Ghaznavids of Afghanistan.

THE MONGOL INVASION

Early in the 13th century the Mongols under Genghis Khan swept out of the steppes of Central Asia and first over-ran China (1211–14), then in 1220 advanced westward against the Empire of Khwarizm (modern Iran, Turkestan and north-western India). Before he died in 1227, Genghis had conquered a vast territory from the Black Sea to Korea. In a series of lightning campaigns his immediate successors conquered most of Russia and, by 1241, had advanced into Poland and Hungary. By 1260 the Mongol Empire was divided among the descendants of Genghis and out of this developed separate dynasties in Siberia and the

Above: A Kay-Khusraw II type drachm (top) shows Byzantine influences, and the distinctive concentric design of an 11th-century Fatimid dinar (middle) is reflected in an anonymous silver dirham of the Golden Horde (bottom).

Above: An 18th-century Ottoman coin of Osman III.

Below: An Islamic street scene with a porter and a metalworker.

Crimea, and most notably in China under Kublai Khan. Their impact on coinage was considerable. They generally made use of the coins they seized as booty, or made crude copies of them, but later the khans of the Golden Horde produced small silver coins distinguished by their inscriptions, while the Ilkhans of Persia struck handsome coins in gold, silver and bronze reciting their titles and family tree. They did not contribute to European coinage and their impact on Islamic coins was slight, though coins of the Seljuks of Rum, struck at Qonya, include the adjective *mahrusat* ("well-defended" – against the menace from the east).

SELJUQS OF RUM

In 1055 Tughril Beg the Seljuq seized Baghdad and founded a dynasty that eventually controlled most of Anatolia, otherwise known as Asia Minor or Rum ("land of the Romans"). The Seljuqs of Rum were the most powerful of the Turkmen tribes and eventually prevailed over the others, establishing their capital at Qonya. In turn, they were defeated by the Mongols but remained significant until the early 14th century, producing a vast

---

Islamic Calendar

Most Islamic coins are dated from the Hegira, the flight of Muhammad from Mecca to Medina in AD 622. The Islamic calendar consists of 12 lunar months (as opposed to solar, or luni-solar), so it falls shorter than the Gregorian year. The date 1201, below, equates to 1786 in the Gregorian calendar.

Above: Modern coins of Islamic countries often show the ruler, as in this Iraqi coin of the 1950s portraying King Faisal II (top). Square silver dirhams of Morocco (bottom), a type introduced by Abd al-Mumin c. AH 550, were popular for 250 years.

series of coins mostly distinguished by square frames within a circle. Coins of a similar type were struck by the Mamluks of Egypt.

As Seljuq power declined, the Turkic tribes of western Anatolia became more independent, and distinctive coins were struck by the Qaramanids from about 1300, and the Jandarids soon after. Coins were also minted by the Sarukhan, Isfendiyarids and Eretnids, before the emergence of the Ottomans about 1350 under Bayazid bin Murad. His son Suleyman was the first Ottoman ruler to adopt the *toughra* or sign-manual of the sultan as a coin symbol; it survives in some Arab coinage to this day.

OTTOMAN EMPIRE

The Ottoman rulers of Turkey and western Asia began minting coins in the 15th century in gold, silver and bronze, featuring the toughra of the ruler and inscriptions in Arabic script. This type of coinage continued in Turkey until 1933, when the lira of 100 kurus was adopted. The portrait of Kemal Ataturk then began to grace the coins, emphasizing Turkey's transformation into a secular country, and henceforward inscriptions were in the modified Roman alphabet.

ISLAMIC COINS TODAY

Egypt, Morocco and the Yemen all have a long history of distinctive coins, clinging to Islamic tradition with lengthy inscriptions in place of portraiture, and numerous variations of the Bismillah ("There is no God but God and Muhammad is His Prophet"). Morocco's main concession to symbolism was the inclusion of the national emblem, a five-pointed star. All these countries have now adopted portraiture. By contrast, Saudi Arabia retains strong conservative traditions. It used Ottoman coinage until distinctive coins were minted in the early 1900s, apart from a few small copper pieces minted at Mecca from 1804. Foreign coins, notably the Maria Theresia thaler of Austria, were countermarked in Arabic.

Persian coins followed the Arab pattern, but under the reforming Shah Nasr-ed-Din (1829–96) a central mint was established at Tehran and coins on European lines were introduced.

Below: An early 20th-century dinar of Saudi Arabia.

INDIAN COINAGE

The Indian subcontinent developed a distinctive coinage, although at various periods it was influenced by political and artistic developments in other parts of the ancient world. Very little is known about hundreds of dynasties other than what can be gleaned from their coins. Ancient languages, such as Kharoshthi, have been deciphered from bilingual Indo-Greek coins.

EARLY INDIAN CURRENCIES

The earliest coins appeared *c.* 500 BC, when silver from Persia and Afghanistan began to flow into India. They were irregular in shape but of uniform weight. The use of such symbols as hills, trees, animals and human figures suggests issue by royal authority, rather than merchants' marks.

Coins recovered from a hoard at Mathura in central India, bearing up to seven punch marks, are regarded as the earliest known. Around the same time Taxila, which traded with Mesopotamia, produced curved ingots with punch marks at either end. Most punch-marked coins conform to the Karshapana standard weight of 32 rattis (1 ratti being 11mg/0.17 grains, the weight of a gunja seed). From the presence of coins of Alexander the Great in Indian hoards it appears that punch-marked coins continued long after the advent of Indo-Greek coins in the 4th century BC. Many were circular, showing the influence of Greek models. Later types included copper coins, relatively thick and often square, with various symbols punched on both sides.

Below: A conical copper currency item of ancient India bears designs also found on Mauryan coins.

Above: Indo-Greek tetradrachms and staters struck by the kings of Bactria.

HELLENISTIC COINS

Alexander the Great began his conquest of India in 327 BC and subjugated the territory as far as the Indus before his death in 323, when his vast empire was divided among his generals. Seleucus Nicator seized Persia, Bactria (Afghanistan) and Syria, and struck gold staters and silver tetradrachms, combining Greek and Indian inscriptions. He was checked by a powerful Maurya state ruled by Chandragupta, who married a daughter of Seleucus.

The Mauryan Empire covered most of India beyond the limits of Greek penetration and struck distinctive coins until its disintegration in 180 BC. Many other kingdoms and dynasties

Below: Allegorical subjects on Kushan coins range from Graeco-Roman figures such as Nike to the Hindu god Shiva.

(such as the Satavahanas, Kshatrapas and Maitrakas) then emerged, each producing its own coins. In southern India the best known coinage was that of the Ardhras, who used lead coins inscribed with native characters.

After the death of Seleucus in 281 BC, his empire broke up into several kingdoms, which continued with Indo-Greek coinage. Arsaces became king of Parthia, while Diodotus seized Bactria in 256 BC. The gold staters and copper tetradrachms of Bactria had inscriptions in both Greek and Prakrit. This Indo-Greek kingdom continued for more than a century before it was absorbed into the Kushan Empire.

The Kushans were a nomadic people of north-western China who moved into the Oxus valley in AD 78 and ruled most of what is now Afghanistan, Pakistan and north-west India. Kushan coins portrayed the ruler on the obverse, with a legend in cursive Greek, while the reverse featured Hindu deities with Sanskrit text. After AD 220 the Kushan Empire disintegrated into

Below: Gold dinars struck by kings of the Kushan.

Princely Coinage

Many Indian princes retained the privilege of striking their own coins until 1947, varying in content and denomination according to the ruler's whim. They range from crude, non-figural pieces to sophisticated coins on Western lines, often produced in London or Birmingham, such as this 1941 silver nazarana rupee of Faridkot, with the bust of Harindar Singh on the obverse and the state arms on the reverse.

numerous petty kingdoms, whose gold dinars and copper coins remained current until the 5th century, latterly with more emphasis on Hindu deities and inscribed in Brahmi script. Were it not for the extraordinary range and beauty of their coins, very little would be known about the Kushans.

THE GUPTAS

A Magadha (Bihar) kingdom, with its capital at Patna, emerged in the late 3rd century AD under Srigupta, founder of a dynasty that lasted for 300 years. His grandson, Chandragupta I (305–25), created the splendid Gupta Empire. The Guptas were noted patrons of the arts and their magnificent coins mirror

Below: Indian Islamic coins include silver horseman tankas of Delhi (bottom) and gold mohurs of the Mughals (right).

their taste, with beautifully executed inscriptions in Sanskrit, written in Brahmi characters. The empire, which extended over most of modern India, had collapsed by 650.

CENTRAL ASIAN INVASIONS

Internal dissension and rebellions made the Gupta Empire easy prey to the Hephthalites or White Huns, migrating westward in the 5th century. From time to time, various local dynasties briefly arose, such as the Vardhanas and Pratiharas, but the poor quality of their coins reflect the dark ages of Indian history under successive invasions.

From 717 to 920 several Turko-Hephthalitic kingdoms occupied what are now Afghanistan and Pakistan, and embraced Hinduism, reflected in the symbolism of their coins. Conversely, by the 9th century, many different coins in central India also reflected the influence of Islam, with motifs derived from Turkic and Sasanian coins, often combined with Hindu deities. In the 10th century various Hindu rulers founded petty kingdoms and minted their own coins, often depicting a seated goddess or a bull and horseman, the latter being a type popularized by the Rajput kingdoms.

ISLAMIC COINS

Arab penetration of India began in the 8th century, and by the end of the 9th century they had conquered Afghanistan, Baluchistan and the Punjab. Mahmud of Gazni (998–1030) raided India and struck silver dirhams at Lahore, with Arabic inscriptions on the obverse but Sanskrit text in Devanagri script on the reverse.

Muhammad Ghori (1173–1206) and his successor Qutub-ud-din Aibak created the Sultanate of Delhi. Qutub, originally a slave, founded the so-called Slave Dynasty, which welded together the petty kingdoms and laid the foundations of the mighty Mughal Empire. In the 13th and 14th centuries crude silver and gold tankas were struck, the forerunners of the beautiful gold and silver coins in which the Arabic script is particularly fine. They often bore verses of Persian poetry, and sometimes the signs of the zodiac. From the beginning of the 18th century, the quality of Mughal coins deteriorated. As the empire broke up, petty rulers began producing their own coins, a privilege that continued under British rule.

India holds the record for the world's largest coins, the stupendous gold 1000 mohurs of Shah Jahangir, struck at Agra in 1613, which weighed over 12kg/26lb. India also produced some of the smallest, the pinhead-sized gold coins of Colpata, weighing only 1 grain (65mg).

Below: A Parthian-style coin with a bearded king and a fire temple.

Above: A Gupta dinar with a king drawing his bow at a rearing tiger.

MINTS

The modern mint is a large complex of secure buildings, but early mints were little more than smithies equipped with a furnace for melting gold and silver, moulds for casting blanks, and hammers and anvils for striking the coins.

As soon as coinage came into being, representing the wealth and power of a country as well as providing a means of trade, coins assumed considerable importance. Reflecting the prestige of the ruler as well as creating commercial confidence, they had to be struck to exact specifications with clearly defined images and inscriptions. This could best be achieved in a central workshop, or provincial workshops using equipment supplied by a central authority. A typical mint, until the advent of mechanization in the 16th century, might consist of a small team of men engaged in melting and refining the raw metal, beating it into sheets and cutting it into roughly circular pieces, which were finally struck as coins by the hammermen. The anvils, with their coining irons (dies), were simple in design, and the equipment could be moved from place to place as occasion demanded.

As trade expanded and demand for coins grew, royal powers and privileges were often devolved to mint-masters or moneyers. In medieval Europe there was a proliferation of local mints, as the privilege of striking coins often passed to feudal lords and Church prelates.

Below: Solidi of Constans, struck at the Siscia Mint (left), and Valentinian III with the mark of the Ravenna Mint.

Above: A 2nd-century Roman coin shows Moneta holding scales and a cornucopia (top); a Phoenician tetrashekel of the Sidon Mint (middle); and half groats of Henry VII, produced by the ecclesiastical Canterbury Mint.

This trend was reversed in the 16th century as government became more centralized, and the coining privilege was restricted to the Crown.

AN ANCIENT TERM

The word "mint" is derived from the Latin word *moneta*, because the place where Roman coins were originally struck was the temple of the goddess Juno Moneta (literally Juno who monitors or warns) on the northern peak of the Capitoline Hill. The goddess had earned her nickname because she was said to have warned the Romans not to undertake any but just wars, promising in return that they would never run

Above: The 15th-century Austrian Emperor Maximilian I is given a tour of a German mint.

short of money. Moneta was personified in Roman myth and was usually depicted on Roman coins as a woman holding a balance and a cornucopia, or horn of plenty. Many Roman coins, from the reigns of Caracalla to Valens, have a reverse showing three figures of Moneta, holding scales and cornucopiae with lumps of gold, silver and bronze at their feet.

The name Moneta was later used to signify the workshop attached to the temple, and the bronze asses coined there were known as *monetae*. This use of the same term to describe pieces of money and the place where they were produced continues today in many European languages. In German, for example, the word *Münze* is used for "coin", "money" and "mint", and

Siege Pieces

During the English Civil War, the besieged Royalist stronghold of Newark-on-Trent was one of four towns with a temporary mint. It issued pieces of silver plate cut into diamond shapes and stamped on one side with the crown and monogram of Charles I above the value in Roman numerals (30 pence). The reverse bore OBS (for the Latin *obsidium*, "siege") above the name of the town and the date.

Dutch *munt* and Swedish *mynt* have the same meanings. In the Romance languages the same word is used for coin and money but not the mint. Thus, French *monnaie*, Italian *moneta*, Spanish *moneda* and Portuguese *moeda* can all mean "coin" or "money", but "mint" is *hotel de monnaie*, *zecca*, *casa de moneda* and *casa da moeda* respectively. In English, "money", "monetary" and "mint" come from the same root. The word "coin" comes from the French word for a corner, which is derived from the Latin *cuneus*, a wedge.

ANCIENT MINTS AND MINT-MARKS

The names, abbreviated or in full, of the places where coins were issued began with Athens ("Athe") inscribed on coins of the 5th century BC, but it was not until the time of Alexander the Great that mint names were explicitly marked. By the end of the 4th century BC, standardization of coin types throughout the empire was the norm, and coins of the same design might be struck in many different mints. The coins of Alexander from Damascus and the Phoenician mints at Sidon and Akko, however, bore inscriptions that

Above: The circular symbol above the 'M' on this 18th-century Spanish reverse distinguishes the Mexico City mint from the Casa de Moneda, Madrid.

identified them. This system was revived by the Romans from the time of Probus (AD 276–82), the abbreviated names or initials of mints usually appearing in the exergue (the separate area below the design) on the reverse.

The Romans operated a highly complex system. Those cities that enjoyed the coining privilege had establishments that consisted of one or more monetary workshops (*officinae monetae*). On the coins of Valentinian II, Valens and Gratian in the 4th century the *officinae* were often designated by the letters P, S, T or Q (*prima*, *secunda*, *tertia* and *quarta*, denoting first, second, third or fourth). These letters may be found on their own in the field (the background of the design), in the exergue or before or after the initials of the mint town.

Mints in the Western Empire generally had a few *officinae*, though Rome had as many as 12. In the Eastern Empire, mints were much larger, and Constantinople had up to 11, while Antioch had 15 and Alexandria 19. Eastern workshops were sometimes denoted by 'OFF' on coins, followed by Roman numerals or Greek letters.

MEDIEVAL TO MODERN

After the fall of the Roman Empire in the west, European coin production was reduced to bare essentials, reflected in crude designs and irregular shapes. Early medieval production was split between numerous small workshops, and every town of any size had at least one. Over a thousand locations have been recorded in inscriptions found on the gold triens of Merovingian France.

In medieval England the names of mints were included on the reverse of coins from the 10th century onwards and at least 109 place names have been identified on Anglo-Saxon, Norman and early Plantagenet coins. Thereafter production became more centralized, and the number of mints decreased.

A similar pattern applied to other European countries in the same period. Medieval Germany consisted of many kingdoms, principalities and duchies, each with its own mint. Today, Germany is the only European country to divide production between several mints, in Berlin, Hamburg, Karlsruhe, Munich and Stuttgart. The United States has operated eight mints at various times since 1793, many of which have now ceased production.

Below (clockwise from top-left): Souvenir medals commemorating the assay office of New York and mints of San Francisco and Denver. (Bottom-left): The Royal Canadian mint has branches at Ottawa and Winnepeg (pictured), the former minting collector coins, the latter circulating coins.

COMMON CURRENCY AND TRADE COINS

There is a scene in Stevenson's *Treasure Island* in which Jim Hawkins and his mother sort through the possessions of the old buccaneer who has died at their inn. Mrs Hawkins wishes to collect what he owed her in board and lodging. "'I'll have my dues, and not a farthing over,'" she says as they count the coins: "It was a long, difficult business, for the coins were of all countries and sizes – doubloons, and louis-d'ors, guineas, and pieces of eight, and I know not what besides, all shaken together at random."

Above: A Mercia penny (top) and a 13th-century Scandinavian imitation of a radiate-type penny.

Below: Hernán Cortés and his Spanish troops discover Aztec treasure.

This sentence vividly conveys the manner in which coins of many countries were widely accepted because of the purity of their gold or silver content. This was not a new phenomenon, for certain gold and silver coins of ancient Greece circulated far beyond the boundaries of the cities that issued them. The Turtles of Aegina, the Foals of Corinth and above all the Owls of Athens were readily accepted all over the Mediterranean and probably even further afield, if the evidence of coin hoards is to be believed. Roman denarii and aurei, the staters and didrachms of Macedon and the darics and sigloi of Persia ranked among the leading trade coins of the ancient world.

From the time of King Offa of Mercia the English silver penny was prized for its high production values and metal content. The adjective "sterling", meaning of the highest character, is derived from the silver penny, which was 92.5 per cent pure. To this day sterling silver is an alloy of 925 parts silver to 75 parts copper, a composition that makes for great durability. The popularity of the penny caused some consternation for the local economy, however. As these good quality coins

Above: A speciedaler of Christiania (Oslo) of 1663 (top) and a jefimok rouble of Russia, counterstamped on a Salzburg thaler of 1625 (bottom).

began increasingly to drain abroad, periodic shortages resulted in England itself, and conversely the country was prone to invasions of poor quality imitations, known as pollards or crockards, from continental Europe. Successive monarchs were perplexed by the mixed blessing of producing a strong currency.

THE MIGHTY DOLLAR

The history of the world's most popular coin is an interesting one. Its origins are not in the New World but in an obscure valley in Bohemia (now part of the Czech Republic). Jachymov was known in German as Joachimsthal, and it was near this town, in 1519, that a large strike of silver was made. The Counts of Schlick coined the metal into large coins known as guldengroschen, which came to be nicknamed Joachimsthalers. Shortened to "thaler", the name was adopted for a wide range of large German silver coins, ranging from 60 to 72 kreuzer in value, some beautifully inscribed, which survived until 1872. The name was corrupted in other languages to talar (Saxony), tallero (Italy), tolar (Slovenia), talari (Ethiopia), tala (Samoa), dala (Hawaii),

daalder (Netherlands), daler (Denmark and Sweden) and dollar. The term "dollar" was first used in Scotland for the 30 shilling piece of James VI in 1567–71, while coins denominated in dollars and fractions of a half, quarter, eighth and sixteenth were struck at Edinburgh in the reign of Charles II (1676–82), long before the dollar became the standard unit of currency in the American colonies. Just to be different, the Russians adapted the first part of the original name (Joachim) for their large silver coins, jefimki (singular *jefimok*).

The thaler crossed the Atlantic in the form of the crude but vigorous silver coins minted in the Spanish colonies. The silver was cast into circular bars which were sliced to form "cobs" that could be stamped with the Spanish regal device. These were the coins that Jim Hawkins referred to as "pieces of eight" – *pesos a ocho reales* (literally, a weight of 8 reals or bits). The American silver dollar became almost as popular as its Spanish counterpart,

Above: British trade dollars of the Bombay Mint (top) and an 1852 silver peso of Bolivia (bottom).

although it was its paper equivalent that conquered the world and is the only truly international currency of the present time.

SILVER TRADE DOLLARS

To challenge the supremacy of the Spanish peso, England introduced a trade dollar in 1600, when its "merchant adventurers" were setting out to establish trade in Muscovy (Russia) and the Indies. British trade dollars, mainly circulating in China and the Far East, continued to be struck at the Royal Mint until World War II.

The United States also minted trade dollars for use in the Pacific, rivalling the beautiful pesos of Mexico, which were so pure that the silver was soft and easily knocked. The Chinese, who used these foreign coins for large transactions, eventually produced silver yuan, or dollars, of their own, which were likewise traded readily all around the Pacific area.

GOLD TRADE COINS

Certain gold coins achieved world popularity that endured for many centuries. From the late medieval period, the florins of Florence and the ducats of Venice were traded internationally and

they inspired similar coins in the Netherlands, Austria and Hungary down to recent times. From 1816, however, the preferred gold coin was the British sovereign.

BULLION COINS

Coins struck in gold, silver or platinum, whose value is not determined by any inscription as such but by the weight and fineness usually inscribed on them, are known as bullion coins. Their value depends on the prevailing price of precious metals in the leading world markets on any particular day. They came to prominence in the 20th century, when gold and silver disappeared from everyday currency, affording a means of trading in these metals on a small scale. Thus, the Mexican 50 peso coin, known as the Libertad, was re-issued from 1943, with the value omitted and its weight and fineness substituted. This was the forerunner of the Krugerrand (South Africa), followed by the Maple Leaf (Canada), the Panda (China), the Nugget (Australia), the Angel (Isle of Man) and the Britannia series (Britain).

Below: The popular six-ducati of Naples and Sicily, 1768 (top). Under Queen Victoria, the British sovereign (middle) became the world's most widely traded gold coin. Today, common currency in the form of the euro (bottom) encourages trade between member countries.

Doubloons

The English term "doubloon" was widely, but loosely, applied to many Spanish-Mexican gold coins, which poured into Europe from the 16th century onward. It was derived from the Spanish *doblone*, the augmentative of *dobla* ("double"), which was applied originally to the 2 escudo denomination.

MONEY OF NECESSITY

From time to time in history, proper coins have been either in short supply or non-existent. Such situations often arose in wartime, because people tended to hoard good gold and silver coins. Wars and civil conflicts also gave rise to situations where towns were besieged and the governor or garrison commander resorted to temporary measures to pay his troops. More often than not, however, it was an economic crisis that drove coins out of circulation, leading merchants and tradesmen to take matters into their own hands and issue tokens.

INTRINSIC VERSUS NOMINAL VALUE

A token is any piece of money whose intrinsic value is less than its face value. In that sense all modern coins are tokens, because their metallic worth is almost invariably less than their nominal, legal tender value. Until the 19th century, however, most countries issued coins that contained metal up to the value at which they circulated.

This applied mainly to gold and silver, but it should be noted that Britain's first copper penny and 2 pence (1797) were very cumbersome because they contained 1 and 2 ounces of metal respectively, copper being then valued

Above: British tokens often imitated the designs of real coins: a George and Dragon freehouse token reading, "At the George in Cheapside Markett" (top), a Sussex halfpenny token (middle), and a Suffolk 1s 6d (bottom).

at a penny an ounce (28g). The difference between real and nominal value has widened over the years, with the debasement of silver coins and finally the complete replacement of silver by cupro-nickel and other base alloys. Conversely, there have been instances of small copper or bronze coins having a greater intrinsic worth than their face value and actually costing twice as much to produce as they were worth in circulation.

FILLING THE GAP

Token coinage was either sanctioned or permitted in ancient Greece and Rome, and was struck by many towns for local circulation. Tokens were generally made of copper or even lead and used for small change. They are of immense interest, as they often bear symbols and images of purely local significance.

Many of the small civic coins of the Middle Ages really come into the same category, although they have attained

Protest Piece

This imitation of the Cartwheel penny of 1797 bears the inscription: "No landlords you fools/ Spence's Plan for ever". The reference is to Thomas Spence (1750–1814), the pioneer of agrarian socialism, who published a pamphlet in 1801 attacking the great landowners. Spence was convicted of seditious libel, fined £20 and sentenced to a year in prison. He also produced the "Hive of Liberty" trade token in 1793.

the status of coins. In many European countries, notably France, Germany and Italy, these local coins continued until the 19th century, either officially sanctioned or unofficially condoned because they served a useful purpose. This was also true of the numerous local issues in India and China. Similarly the copper cents and sous that

Below: A citizen exchanging assignats, the paper notes that replaced coinage during the French Revolution.

Below: A Roman provincial coin struck at Tyre during the reign of Hadrian (top); an Abbasid coin struck by a local governor, under the caliphate but in his own district (bottom).

Above: An Anglesey copper halfpenny of 1788 (left) and an Irish silver 10 pence bank token, 1805 (right).

were circulating in Canada before Confederation in 1867 are regarded as coins, although they were issued by the various provincial banks.

BRITISH TOKENS

As money of necessity, tokens cast or struck in lead, pewter or copper enjoyed a purely local circulation in England from the early 15th century-onward. These farthings and half farthings were tolerated but had no official sanction. Periodically, the government tried to stamp them out, but as the monarch was reluctant to issue any coins other than in silver or gold, there were times when merchants and shopkeepers were forced to produce tokens to use as small change for the benefit of their customers.

There was such an acute shortage of small coins by the end of the English Civil War in 1649 that tokens proliferated, and it has been estimated that there were more than 4000 different types in London alone. After the Restoration, regal halfpence and farthings were adopted in 1672 and tokens were suppressed by 1674. They were revived in 1787, however, when silver pennies disappeared from general circulation, as small copper coins had

Below: An American tin token of James II, struck in 1688.

not been minted since 1775. The Anglesey Copper Mining Company led the way with its Druid penny, which circulated widely. Over the ensuing decade hundreds of different tokens, mostly halfpence and pennies, were produced by businessmen, merchants and shopkeepers and are of immense social interest on account of their commercial advertising. John Palmer, Mayor of Bath and pioneer of the mail coach, issued a halfpenny that showed his invention on the reverse. Some of the pennies bore an inscription stating that 240 of them could be redeemed for a pound note.

Copper tokens were outlawed in 1797 when the Cartwheel copper pennies were introduced, but a shortage of silver coins during the Napoleonic Wars even led to tokens for 1s 6d and 3 shillings being issued by the Bank of England in the early 19th century. Copper tokens were again issued from 1811 until the 1830s.

AMERICAN TOKENS

Tokens were struck in the American colonies, or imported from private manufacturers in England and Ireland, to fill gaps in the coinage supplied from the mother country, and this continued until the 1790s pending the supply of coins from the US Mint.

Hard Times tokens, also known as Copperheads, appeared in 1834–44 during a shortage of cents and half cents. Many of them bore political slogans reflecting the power struggle between President Andrew Jackson and the Bank of the United States. There was a rash of tokens during the Civil War, often of a patriotic nature, when coins were in short supply. Even postage stamps were pressed into service, encased in small circular discs that carried commercial advertisements on the back.

WARTIME SHORTAGES

During and immediately after World War I, coins were in short supply in France, Germany, Italy and other countries, and this was remedied by the issue

Above: An aluminium-bronze 2 franc token issued by the French chambers of commerce during the economic crisis of 1922–3.

of tokens by chambers of commerce and local authorities, usually recognizable by the inscription "Bon Pour" ("good for") or its equivalent in other languages. Tokens also appeared during the Spanish Civil War (1936–9), including circular discs with stamps affixed to them. In Russia, stamps were reprinted on stout card and had an inscription on the back signifying their parity with small silver coins. Stamps affixed to cards circulated in lieu of coins in Rhodesia during the Boer War, and this practice was followed by some French colonies in World War I and parts of India in World War II.

OBSIDIONAL CURRENCY

From the Latin word *obsidium* ("siege") comes the term for coins produced by the defenders of besieged towns. The first record of this practice comes from the Siege of Tyre during the First Crusade in 1122, when stamped pieces of leather were used as money. Leather coins were also produced at Faenza (1240) and Leiden (1573–4), when the bindings of hymn books were pressed into service. The first metal pieces were uniface lead coins produced in Saint-Omer in 1477.

The issue of siege coins has been recorded on more than 130 occasions and they include silver and even gold pieces crudely cut from commandeered plate and stamped with a mark of value and usually with the civic arms. This custom appears to have been confined to Europe, although paper notes for the same purpose were produced during the sieges of Khartoum (1885) and Mafeking (1900).

PARTS AND PROCESSES

This section looks at the various factors that distinguish coins by type and value, and the different techniques used to produce them. We also investigate the history of counterfeiting coins and the security features that have evolved to combat the circulation of bogus coins and imitations, like this one shilling and sixpence token of 1811, produced in Suffolk, England.

DENOMINATIONS

Traditionally, the denomination of a coin was determined solely by the weight and fineness, and thus the intrinsic value, of the metal used. We have already touched upon the weight systems based on the ancient Greek talent or Roman libra, but many other value systems were used in antiquity.

One of the earliest was based on the *shoti* of the Middle East, weighing about 120 grains. The grain, still used in weights and measures today, was derived from a grain of barley. The unit of weight in Egypt was the *deben*, made up of 10 *qedets*, and numerous qedet weights have been discovered not only

Below: In The Banker and his Wife, *by the 15th-century Flemish artist Quentin Metsys, the husband counts and weighs his gold coins while his wife studies a book of devotions.*

in Egypt but also at Troy and at Knossos in Crete. The system of weights that evolved in Mesopotamia was used across the Persian Empire throughout Asia Minor, Greece, southern Italy and as far west as Ireland in pre-Roman times. In this system 60 um made a sikkur, 6 sikkur a shekel, 60 shekels a maneh and 60 maneh a talent.

MONEY OF ACCOUNT

Broadly speaking, all monetary systems (including money of account) are based on the relationship of one unit to another. In Britain, for example, 12 copper pennies were worth 1 silver shilling and 20 silver shillings were worth one gold sovereign or pound. It is usually convenient to use different metals to express this relationship, but

Above: During the 11th and 12th centuries, British silver pennies were often simply cut in half to accommodate the need for small change in everyday commercial transactions.

the ratio of one to another has differed over the centuries in many parts of the world. Often, different denominations

Gold Guineas

The guinea was first issued in 1663 under Charles II (below); its name arose because much of the gold came from Guinea in Africa. It was valued at 20 shillings, but this increased as the price of gold rose. The last guinea was issued in 1813, as the "Great Recoinage" of 1816 replaced it with the pound, though it continued as money of account, valued at 21 shillings, until 1971.

Below: A Roman aes grave, marked with heads of barley and pellets.

Above: A sixpence of Charles II with interlocking Cs.

Above: Gold oban and koban coins being marked in 18th-century Japan.

evolved from the earliest monetary systems. The £sd system used in Britain until 1971 was derived from the Roman system, in which the libra was divided into 20 solidi or 240 denarii. Adopted by the Carolingian Empire, this survived in many European countries. Pre-Revolutionary France had the livre of 20 sols or 240 deniers, while Italy had the lira of 20 soldi or 240 denari.

In Germany, by contrast, the mark was divided into 4 vierding, 16 loth, 32 setin, 64 quentchen, 256 richtpfennig or 512 heller, but only the pfennig and heller existed as coins. However, all these units could be used as "money of account". The latter is, as its name suggests, any unit employed in the keeping of accounts: it is sometimes represented by actual coins but quite often not.

Above: George III shillings of 1787 and 1817 (back left and right), and silver Maundy pennies marked, unusually for the period, with Arabic numerals.

Just as metric and imperial systems are concurrent today, multiple value systems sometimes existed in the same country. In the later medieval period England had gold coins in different finenesses: 22 carat was used for the sovereign (20 shillings), half sovereign (10 shillings) and crown (5 shillings), but 23.5 carat for the noble (6s 8d) and its sub-divisions. The gold guinea (21 shillings) was replaced by the sovereign in 1816 but remained as money of account until the advent of decimal currency in 1971.

The denominations within each system were relative to each other, but different values could be attributed to the same units in different systems. In France the livre was worth 2 marks, but in England the mark was equivalent to two-thirds of a pound, both in weight (8 ounces) and value (13s 4d).

MARKS OF VALUE

The earliest coins bore no mark of value: this was implicit in their size and weight. Most Roman coins were undenominated apart from the aes grave, on which different values were indicated by varying numbers of pellets. Some Byzantine gold coins were inscribed OB, followed by Greek letters forming the number 72. This was an abbreviation for *obruson* ("pure"), and indicated that the coins had been struck at the rate of 72 to the pound of pure metal. Roman numerals XII, XXI or XLII

may be found on Vandal coinage to indicate denominations, while some English silver coins of Tudor and Jacobean times were inscribed with Roman numerals behind the monarch's head to denote their values in shillings or pence.

MULTIPLE DENOMINATIONS

Most countries get by with six or eight coins in everyday circulation. Before the general advent of paper money to represent higher values, coins played a much more prominent role, hence the need for high-denomination coins in gold and silver. Today the number of different coins in general use tends to be governed by the lowest paper denomination that is practical (which is dependent on the average life of a banknote). In Britain, for example, this is now £5: eventually the note may be replaced by a coin, as the life of a £5 note is only about three months.

The USA is virtually unique in persevering with a $1 bill (worth about 1 euro), whereas in Europe coins of 1 euro and 2 euros are in everyday use. Lower denominations merely serve the purpose of small change. Such factors as payment of taxes and the facilitation of trade, formerly served by large silver or gold coins, are now entirely supplied by paper or electronic bank transfer.

METALS AND ALLOYS

With very few exceptions, coins are made of metal. Pure, unadulterated metals are seldom used, although even the ancient Greeks managed to achieve a relatively pure gold for some coins. In the main, two or more metals are combined to form an alloy, giving greater durability. We think of copper, silver and gold as traditional coin metals, but a surprising range of other metals has been employed, ranging from platinum and palladium to pewter, tin, and even relatively dense compositions of lead.

METAL FINENESS

In the ancient world coins were simply pieces of precious metal, which could, of course, be weighed at each transaction. However, it was more convenient to accept the mark stamped on a coin as a guarantee not only of its weight but also its purity. For this reason, units of value were usually tied to specific

Right: A Russian platinum 3 rouble coin of 1830.

Below: Spanish settlers in Mexico smelting mined gold in imitation of the Aztecs.

Above: A Roman gold aureus with a lump of gold added to it to make up the correct weight.

weights and these, in turn, were derived from particular seeds or grains. Nowadays the fineness of precious coinage metals is measured in thousandths, using a much more precise system than the carat used in ancient times, though this unit has been retained in the assessment of jewellery.

ELECTRUM

The earliest coins of the Western world were made of electrum, a natural alloy of about 73 per cent gold and 27 per cent silver, found in riverbeds in the Tmolus Mountains of Lydia (present-day Anatolia in Turkey). Electrum was widely used for the coins of the 6th and 7th centuries BC. Latterly, the Greeks' love of white gold encouraged them to produce an artificial alloy consisting of one part gold and ten parts silver. The Celts copied electrum staters but severely debased them with copper and silver, and the Merovingians produced base electrum coins in which the gold content was minimal.

Theoretically any alloy of gold less than 75 per cent should be described as electrum, but in practice this is confined to classical and medieval coins. Some coins of the Isle of Man were struck in an alloy containing 9 carat gold (.375 fine), when the bullion price of gold was exceptionally high.

GOLD

The most popular of the precious metals was preferred by Croesus, King of Lydia (560–546 BC), who abandoned electrum for a bimetallic system with a

Above: A platinum noble (1983) and a deluxe silver coin (1993) struck by the Pobjoy Mint in the Isle of Man.

gold–silver ratio of 40:3 (or 13.3:1). Coins were struck in relative weights, so that one gold piece was worth 20 of silver. This arrangement, fixed by the Lydians and Persians in the 6th century BC, continued in Rome and the Carolingian Empire and survived in Britain until World War I, the gold sovereign being worth 20 silver shillings.

The fineness of gold was based on the carat which, in addition to being a weight, came to represent a 24th part. Thus, pure gold is described as 24 carat fine. The purest gold for medieval coinage was 23 carat 3½ grains (.997 fine), which was as pure as the primitive metallurgy of the period could get. English gold was debased to 20 carat by 1545, but was eventually standardized at 22 carat (.9167 fine), originally

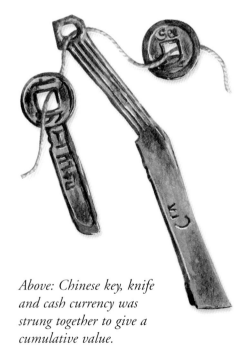

Above: Chinese key, knife and cash currency was strung together to give a cumulative value.

known as "crown gold" due to its first being used for the crown series. It was alloyed with .083 copper to produce a durable alloy with a reddish lustre and continues in the sovereign to this day.

The USA used the same fineness from 1795 to 1834 but later settled on .900. Mexico preferred .875, while France and Germany opted for .900 fine. The world's first major bullion coin of recent times, the Krugerrand, was minted to .9167 standard (the most practical and hard-wearing fineness), but later bullion coins strove for the utmost purity. Canada achieved .999 pure gold for the Maple Leaf (1979), but improved refining techniques led to the famous "four nines" gold first used in 1983. Bullion coins have both the weight and fineness of the metal inscribed on them.

SILVER

Used for coinage by the mid-6th century BC, mainly for the drachma and its sub-divisions, silver remained the preferred medium for the denarius, the denier and the penny, as well as most of the everyday coins of the world until the middle of the 20th century.

Medieval silver was .958 pure but was too soft to be practical, and .925 silver was the widely used sterling standard, usually alloyed with .075 copper. On many occasions, however, governments resorted to debasement of silver. Mexico, for example, struck coins in .903 silver until 1905 but, under pressure from inflation, then progressively debased it to .420 (1935), .300 (1950) and finally .100 (1957– 67). Low-grade silver alloys are often described as

Below: The "Rosa Americana" (1722), a British colonial brass 2 pence, was cheaply minted and consequently rejected by the American colonists.

Above: Wartime shortages led to the use of base metals for this Norwegian coin of the German occupation (top) and Belgian zinc 5 cents of 1915 (bottom).

billon. While base alloys are now used for circulating coinage, de luxe and collectors' coins are generally struck in silver of a high quality.

BASE METALS

As copper was tariffed at 3000 to 1 piece of gold, it was very cumbersome, and for that reason it was seldom used for coins at its intrinsic value. The strings of Chinese cash are an example; the enormous copper plates of 17th-century Sweden, known as plåtmynt, are another. More or less pure copper was used for subsidiary coins in Britain from the 17th century until 1860, but then the size was reduced and the copper alloyed with tin to form bronze. A small amount of zinc is often added.

Brass is an alloy of 80 per cent copper and 20 per cent zinc, used by the Romans and revived by Switzerland during World War I. Modern brass coins are alloys of bronze with aluminium or nickel. Aluminium, noted for its lightness, was first used in British West Africa (1/10 penny) and British East Africa (half cent and cent) in 1907–8. Adopted as an emergency measure in Europe during World War I and revived in World War II, it has since become much more widespread, usually for the lowest denominations.

Nickel has been used in coins since the 3rd century BC but was adopted by Belgium in 1860 as a substitute for billon in the smallest coins. Pure nickel coins have been used as a substitute for silver in many European countries. Although Canada is the largest producer of nickel, it did not use it in coins until 1922, when nickel replaced silver in the 5 cent coin. The USA adopted an alloy of 75 per cent copper and 25 per cent nickel ("cupro-nickel") for the 3 cent coin of 1865. Cupro-nickel 5 cents appeared in 1866 and circulated alongside silver half dimes until 1873. The 5 cent coin is still popularly known as a nickel, but since 1964 this metal has also been used for the dime and higher denominations.

BIMETALLIC AND CLAD COINS

Clad coins have a core of one metal and an outer layer in another, such as stainless steel clad with copper (like most pennies and cents today).

Bimetallic coins have a centre in one metal and an outer ring in another. Tin farthings of Charles II (1684–5) had a copper plug in the middle. In the 19th century there were experiments with base metal coins with a silver plug to raise their intrinsic value. Since Italy pioneered bimetallic coins in 1982, alloys of gold and silver colour have been widely used for higher denominations. There are even trimetallic coins, but generally the central "plug" is of the same metal as the outer ring.

Coins on a Coin

This large gold-on-silver bimetallic coin from the Isle of Man reproduces an entire series of Cat crowns issued over the previous ten years.

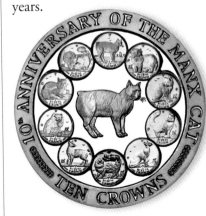

SPECIFICATIONS

All coins are produced within particular parameters. As well as the purity of the metal or alloy, they must conform to particular weights, and certain specifications such as diameter and thickness. As well as the conventional round shape, many coins are polygonal or scalloped, with or without a central hole – all features that help users to distinguish the different denominations.

THICKNESS

In general, thick coins were common in ancient times because they started life as lumps of precious metal of a particular weight, which were cast in moulds and then struck. Only when the use of sheet metal became more practical were blanks cut with shears, enabling thinner coins to be produced.

Nowadays we are accustomed to coins that are neither too thick nor too thin, that handle easily and stack well. The surface of modern coins is relatively flat and great care is taken in their design to ensure an even balance between the obverse (heads) and reverse (tails). Modern coins have to be stackable in tall piles or, more importantly, operate smoothly in the acceptor–rejector mechanisms of pay-phones, slot machines and automats.

Below: Unusual shapes of modern coins (clockwise from top left) include scalloped (Israel), octagonal (Malta, and Macao) and heptagonal (Jordan).

Above: Silver Tiger Tongue money (top) and Leech money (bottom) from Thailand, and square and diamond-shaped coins of ancient India (middle) .

SHAPE

The earliest coins were small electrum dumps of irregular shape. Some Celtic coins were globular, while the mameita gin of feudal Japan were bean-shaped. Thailand's so-called "bullet money" consisted of silver balls or gold cylinders, which were bent into rough balls.

Chinese sycee currency was given its name (*hsi ssu*, meaning "fine silk") in allusion to the purity of its silver. One form was a thick oblong oval, raised at the ends because it was rocked as the metal was cooled partially, before being stamped with maker's and assayer's marks. Sycee was current from the 8th century AD until 1933, when it was suppressed by the Kuomintang government.

UNUSUAL SHAPES

Oval coins have been produced in Japan and the ancient Persians had elliptical coins. The original kopeks of Russia were made from heavy silver wire, which was cut into short strips,

Above: A gold ingot issued by the Central Mint of China in 1945.

then hammered into ovals. They were extremely light and only about 15mm/ ⅝in long, providing small change from 1534 until about 1700. Many copper farthings of James I and Charles I (1613–42) had an upright oval shape.

Square or rectangular coins were common in Asia from pre-Christian times to the early 20th century. The style was popular in the Indo-Scythian and Indo-Greek coinage of the 2nd century BC, and continued under the Mughal Empire, down to the Indian feudal states. These coins were true squares with sharp corners, but in India and the Far East, modern square coins have rounded corners, which are much more user-friendly. The Netherlands is the only European country to have adopted this shape: 5 cent coins of 1913–40 had a diamond format, followed by a square format in 1941–3.

Rectangular coins were also popular in Asia and ranged from the long, narrow vertical gia long of Annam to the more elegantly proportioned silver cho gin and gold koban of Japan before the Meiji Revolution of the 1860s.

Klippe

Square or lozenge-shaped coins, known as *klippe*, were produced in many of the German states, and the form later spread as far afield as Poland, Hungary and Denmark. These coins were originally struck in times of emergency, when pieces were cut from silver plate, but later the shape became fashionable and coins were made as presentation pieces, with ornament in the corners. Pictured here is a klippe thaler of Friedrich Augustus I of Saxony, issued in 1697.

POLYGONAL COINS

The only true pentagons (with sharp corners) are the 1/16 and 1/8 ahmadi riyals of the Yemen (1947–60), but five-sided coins with rounded corners have been issued by Belize (1981) and the Solomon Islands (1983). Six-sided coins include the 50 cent coins in aluminium, zinc, brass or bronze from Djibouti (1920–2), the brass 2 francs of the Belgian Congo (1943) and Egypt's silver 2 piastres (1944). In all of these a format with flat sides at top and bottom was adopted. Hexagonal coins with points at top and bottom

Below: A Russian denga of the 11th century (top) and a Mongol silver dirham (bottom).

have been issued by the Yemen (1948), Sudan (1981) and the British Virgin Islands (1982–3).

In 1969, the Royal Mint created a 50 pence coin (worth 10 shillings) from the same weight and alloy as the obsolescent half crown, which had a quarter of the value of the new coin. The only variable in design was the shape; the new coin was given seven sides, a shape later extended to the 20 pence. Heptagonal coins later appeared in many Commonwealth countries. Octagonal (eight-sided) coins with flat top and bottom were favoured by some of the German states in the mid-18th century, and have been produced sporadically in more recent times, notably in Senegal (1920) and Egypt (1933).

Octagons with points at the top and bottom have so far been confined to the $50 gold coin commemorating the Pan-Pacific Exposition (1915) and the gold $200 of the Netherlands Antilles (1976). Thailand (1972), Kenya (1973) and Tuvalu (1976–81) have had nine-sided coins, while Colombia (1967), Afghanistan (1979), the Dominican Republic (1983), Jamaica (1976) and Tanzania (since 1971) have had ten-sided coins.

Dodecagons or 12-sided coins are very popular and were pioneered by Britain for the nickel-brass 3 pence of Edward VIII (1936) and subsequent coins of this value until 1967. Just as Britain was abandoning the shape, it was taken up by many other countries, notably Argentina and Australia. When Canada changed the alloy of its 5 cent coin from nickel to tombac brass in 1942, a 12-sided format was adopted and retained until 1962. Its cent switched from circular to dodecagonal in 1982, saving 10.7 per cent in weight – before the change it was costing 2 cents to produce each cent!

Triangular coins with rounded corners have been produced by the Cook Islands and (appropriately) Bermuda, but the only three-sided coin with sharp corners was the 20 centime of Gabon (1883). The 10 centime had an over-all triangular shape but the points were truncated, so that the coin was actually six-sided.

SERRATED OR SCALLOPED EDGES

The Carthaginians and Seleucids had circular coins with serrated edges, but many modern coins have scalloped edges, a useful feature for distinguishing coins of different values but similar sizes. A "nicked" edge is a feature of the brass 20 euro cent, making it distinct from the 50 cent. Burma has even had polygonal scalloped coins.

Many Asian coins (notably Chinese cash) have a central hole, but this feature was not used elsewhere until 1883 (in Bolivia). It is a means of reducing weight and metal while retaining a relatively large diameter and is now widely practised all over the world.

Above: A square Indian rupee of the Indo-Scythian kings.

HAMMERED AND CAST COINAGE

Although a few coins were cast in moulds, most were struck by hand until the late 17th century, relying on the strength of the craftsman to hit the flan with a hammer. This technique sounds extremely crude, but, thanks to the skill of coiners, and the revival of intaglio techniques first developed in the classical world, intricate portraits, emblems and other designs were achieved long before the industrial age.

CAST COINS

In casting, metal is melted and then poured into a mould. The simplest moulds were merely hollows in a bed of fine sand, which produced the small, roughly circular lumps of metal that were then punch marked. Well into the 17th century, flans or blanks for struck coins were cast in this manner, although cutting blanks from thin sheets of metal gradually superseded this. A refinement was to carve a mould from a piece of stone, enabling detailed designs and lettering to be engraved. Double-sided moulds of this kind were used for double-sided coins.

This technique was used exclusively to produce Chinese cash until 1889, and some provinces continued to cast coins as late as 1908. Latterly multiple moulds were employed to cast several coins simultaneously. They resembled

Below: Early Italian cast coin (top); cast Korean bronze cash or mun (bottom).

Multiple Punch Marks

This coin of Asia Minor, dating from around 400–380 BC, shows similar designs on the obverse (crested Athena standing, left) and reverse (Apollo holding a bow). The reverse contains two rectangular countermarks made by the same punch. Early coins often bear various punch marks applied by different authorities to guarantee their value.

a tree with the coins as the fruit at the ends of "branches" created by the channels along which the molten metal flowed. A few of these "trees" have survived intact, but normally the coins were broken off and the rough edges carefully filed.

Cast coins were used in Japan until 1871, Morocco until 1882, Korea until 1888 and Vietnam until the 1930s. They were seldom produced in Europe, but noteworthy exceptions were the first coins of the Isle of Man (1709), where the halfpenny and penny were cast in a foundry at Castletown. These coins can be recognized by the flash marks on the rim and the slight excrescences where the connecting channels of molten metal were broken off. More recent examples are the copies of 8 real coins of Potosi cast by the garrison of Chiloe in South America (1822), coins cast from gunmetal at Terceira in the Azores for Maria II in exile (1829) and Andorran 1, 5 and 10 diners (1984).

The casting technique produced very crude coins compared to struck examples and was latterly used only in extreme cases when more sophisticated coining equipment was not available.

HAMMER AND ANVIL

The hammermen formed one of the most prestigious trade guilds of the Middle Ages, a measure of the importance and value of their skill. Generally, they worked in groups in which individuals were responsible for specific aspects of the process (smelting and refining, moulding the blanks or cutting them from sheet metal rolled out to a uniform thickness). The coining irons were generally supplied by the central government, but engravers sometimes used dies produced locally.

The earliest blanks or "flans" for hammered coins were cast in moulds, a natural progression from the original dumps and globules. The round blank was relatively thick. It was heated to make it malleable, then placed on an anvil of bronze whose face had been engraved with a device (the obverse). The upper die, a punch, was hit by a

Above: A Crusader "knight" follis from the 12th century with the design struck off-centre.

Below: In Venice, coins continued to be struck by hand until the 18th century.

Above: These medieval German hammermen are working individually, but this was not typical: the striking of coins was usually a two-man operation – one to hold the blank on the anvil with pincers and the other to hammer.

hammer to raise the design on the coin. Subsequently, a metal block with the reverse device engraved on its lower face was placed over the coin and struck, thus producing a double-sided coin. Later, blanks were cut from sheets of metal and roughly trimmed to shape with large shears. This method of coining continued in Europe until the 17th century and survived in some parts of the world until the 1950s.

The dies were normally lined up so that both obverse and reverse designs were vertical, but in many cases an upset position, or alignment of 180 degrees, was preferred – a custom that prevails in many countries to this day. Nevertheless, because coins were struck by hand, it is not uncommon to find the obverse at right angles to the reverse, or some variation to the left or right of the normal upright position.

PILE AND TRUSSEL
By the 11th century a more advanced technique was beginning to evolve in France and Germany, though it did not completely supplant the traditional method until the 17th century. The

"pile and trussel" method avoided progressive wear on the face of the hammer and the need to engrave the die on to the anvil by using dies engraved on pieces of iron or steel.

The pile (bearing the obverse) had a spike on the end, which could be driven into a large tree stump, before which sat the coiner, who then positioned the hot, malleable flan on the pile with a pair of tongs. The trussel, or reverse die, was then positioned over the flan. The hammerman used great force to strike impressions simultaneously into both sides of the coin.

One refinement was the use of tongs or pincers with circular ends, which held the blank and trussel in position on the pile. The force of striking made the metal spread and flow, but the tips of the tongs formed a collar around the blank, which kept the coin reasonably circular in shape. However, the creation of a circular coin with nicely centred images depended entirely on the skill of the hammerman. Many ancient and medieval coins have off-centre images, and these "mis-strikes" are highly prized by some collectors.

DIES AND ENGRAVING
The dies used in coining have evolved through the ages. Those used by the Greeks were engraved on a very hard, durable bronze with a high tin content. The Romans, however, pioneered the

use of iron dies, and occasionally used steel, though this did not become the norm until the 15th century.

The intaglio technique of die-cutting, perfected over many centuries, developed in the ancient civilizations of Egypt, Greece and Rome, primarily for the carving of gems and seals. It must have seemed a logical extension to carve into a piece of iron planed smooth to create the indented image necessary for a coin. The technique of direct engraving reached its peak during the Roman Empire and resulted in coins of remarkable beauty. Like most other arts, it vanished during the Early Medieval period and was not revived in western Europe until the 11th century, although there were isolated examples, such as the gold penny of Offa of Mercia (759–96), the gold solidus of Louis the Pious (814–40) and the silver deniers of Charlemagne from the Palatine Mint of about 800. Direct engraving continued in the Byzantine Empire and it was from there that it was re-introduced to Western Europe.

An interesting example of the transition between old and new is provided by the silver pfennigs of the Holy Roman Empire of about 1010, in which the images were engraved on to the die, but the coin inscriptions were produced using wedge-shaped punches. Direct engraving was largely responsible for the production of bracteates, the thin, button-like coins used in Germany, Switzerland, Poland and Hungary from the late 12th to 14th centuries.

Below: Quadripartite (four-part) incuse punches on ancient Greek coins.

THE FIRST MILLED COINAGE

Mechanical processes revolutionized coin production in the 16th and 17th centuries, but they evolved over a long period. There was considerable opposition to their adoption, as the mint-workers, especially the hammermen, saw machinery as a serious threat to their traditional jobs.

EARLIEST MILLED COINS
Around 1500, Leonardo da Vinci produced a detailed diagram for a double press, which would produce a perfectly circular coin blank and then strike it. Like many of his inventions, this remained only a drawing for centuries, but in the 1960s IBM constructed a blanking and coining press to his specifications, which is now part of the collection of the Smithsonian Institution in Washington DC.

Donato Bramante, working on the principle of the fruit press, created a screw press that produced blanks in 1506, and in 1550 Max Schwab of Augsburg improved it, making it capable of both blanking and striking coins. A decade earlier he had created a device like a giant mangle, which squeezed out sheets of metal of an even thickness, harnessed to a machine like an enormous cookie-cutter, which cut out circular blanks. Unable to interest the German or Italian mints, Schwab sold his inventions to the French. They established a special plant at the tip of the Ile du Palais in Paris, where the

Right: A French milled coin of Charles III, Duke of Lorraine (1593–1607).

Below: An English milled coin of Elizabeth I (1563).

Above: A pattern shilling of Charles I (top) and Nicolas Briot's first issue milled penny (middle) and second issue milled shilling (bottom).

River Seine produced the power to drive the water mills needed to operate the machinery. It was known as the Moulin des Etuves ("mill of the baths"), as it stood on the original site of the palace spa. It was because of this use of water mills that the new coins came to be described as "milled".

Sample coins, or "patterns", were struck in 1551 and the following year went into general production. But output declined after 1554, due mainly to the entrenched hostility of the hammermen, and in 1563 the mint was ordered to confine its activities to medals. Nevertheless, it was reactivated in 1577 to produce France's first copper coinage, and milled coins were also struck there in 1573 for Henry of Navarre as Lord of Béarn. The early milled coins were distinguished from their hammered counterparts by the evenness of their flans, their perfect impressions and the beauty of the engraving and lettering. That they were not an immediate

success was due not only to the strenuous opposition of vested interests but also to the fact that hammered coins were then much cheaper to produce.

ROLLER PRESSES
In other parts of Europe, the rolling and blanking machinery was operated differently. An alternative technique was devised at Augsburg, a city then at the heart of technological progress. This involved pairs of rollers on which the obverse and reverse dies were engraved. Strips of sheet metal were passed between the rollers under high pressure and took up the impressions of the coins, which were then carefully cut out of the strip.

Roller presses and dies of this type were used at the main Habsburg Mint in Kremnica from 1566. The machinery, perfected at Augsburg, was eventually used throughout the Holy Roman Empire until the late 18th century. Several dies (for up to six thalers or 18 smaller coins) could be engraved on the cylinders side by side; entire sheets of metal could then be passed between the cylinders and the resultant

Above: An Oliver Cromwell milled crown of 1658.

Above: A milled papal testone of 1623–44.

coins cut out after striking. The dies were engraved in a slightly elliptical form to compensate for the curvature of the rollers, so that the finished coins emerged perfectly circular.

Roller dies and presses were phased out after the appointment of Daniel Warou as chief engraver at the Kremnica Mint (1699–1703), for he introduced the screw press and made many improvements to it. The screw press remained in use in the Holy Roman Empire until the 1890s, when it was gradually superseded by the hydraulic press.

Ornament and Safeguard

When milled coins became standard in the British Isles in 1662, Pierre Blondeau applied an edge inscription using a secret process of his own invention. The inscription read "Decus et Tutamen Anno Regni …" ("An ornament and a safeguard in the year of the reign …") followed by the Latin ordinal number, for example "Vicesimo" (twentieth). The first part of the inscription now appears around the edge of the current English pound coin. Scottish and Welsh pounds bear different inscriptions, the latter reading Pleidiol Wyf I'm Gwlad ("I am true to my country").

THE SPREAD OF MILLED COINS

Etienne Bergeron, master of the Moulin des Etuves, was ejected from France in 1559 because he was a Huguenot (Protestant). He fled to Navarre, then a separate kingdom, and in 1562 became master of the mint set up by the Huguenots at Orleans, where he converted church plate into milled coins. In 1561, Eloi Mestrel of the Moulin des Etuves also fled from religious persecution. He went to England, where he installed coining machinery in the Tower of London. The first English milled coins were produced here and appeared in 1561–2, but Mestrel fell foul of the English hammermen and was dismissed in 1572.

In 1586 the mint at Segovia in Spain acquired some roller presses and began producing good quality coins, in stark contrast to the crude hammered coins that continued to pour our of the other Spanish mints. Rolling machines, blanking machines and screw presses also spread to the German states and to Bohemia in the early 17th century, and the production of milled coins received stimulus both from the greater output of silver and the propaganda requirements of the Thirty Years War (1618–48).

Above: A 1632 thaler of Archduke Leopold V of Tirol, struck at Hall Mint.

Above: Mis-strikes continued to occur with milled coinage, as in these shillings of Queen Anne (1709, top) and George III, struck off-collar (1819, bottom).

A second experiment with milled coins took place in England in this period. Nicolas Briot was chief engraver at the Paris Mint from 1606 to 1625. In 1615 he invented the *balancier*, an improved machine for striking coins, but it was rejected by his superiors. Briot fled from Paris in 1625 to escape his creditors, and brought his machinery to England. He was allowed to install his presses at the Tower Mint in 1628 and produced some milled gold in 1631–2 and silver until 1639. Later, his beautifully engraved dies were utilized for coins produced by the traditional hammered process. He himself was sent to Edinburgh in 1635 and installed mill and screw machinery there, which resulted in some excellent but short-lived Scottish milled coins.

The outbreak of the English Civil War in 1642 was a major setback, but in 1649 the Commonwealth government revived the idea and invited Pierre Blondeau from the Paris Mint to London. The result was the milled coinage of 1656–8, portraying Cromwell. Hammered coinage continued after the Restoration (1660), but two years later machinery operated by horsepower was installed – the animals powering a treadmill – and thereafter all English coins were milled. Elsewhere in Europe, milled coinage was now the norm, except in Holland where hammered coinage survived until 1670.

INDUSTRIAL DEVELOPMENTS

Although the first coining machinery made use of waterpower and horsepower, the advent of steam, and later electricity, totally transformed the production of coins. The maximum output by horsepower was about 40 coins a minute. Steam presses immediately doubled that rate and today's high-speed electric presses can produce over 700 coins a minute.

STEAM-POWERED MACHINERY
Matthew Boulton and James Watt invented milling and blank-cutting machinery powered by steam. It was installed in 1786 at their Soho Mint in Birmingham, where it was used to strike coins of the East India Company and many British trade tokens. This mint struck the British Cartwheel pennies of 1797, followed by Manx coins in 1798–1813. In 1809 the firm began supplying the Royal Mint with steam-powered machinery, which was first actually used in the "Great Recoinage" of 1816–17. Boulton also started negotiations with the US Mint in 1799, but it was not until 1816 that steam-powered machinery was installed at the Philadelphia Mint.

Right: The "Cartwheel" copper pennies of 1797 were named for their broad rims.

Below: A 1797 illustration of a coining press, dies and a machine designed to engrave coin edges.

Above: These coining presses, photographed in 1910, were capable of striking up to 120 coins per minute.

HIGH-SPEED PRESSES
In 1817, Dietrich Uhlhorn of Grevenbroich, near Cologne, invented the automatic, high-speed coining press. A year later he demonstrated his knuckle-joint knee-lever press at Dusseldorf. Between 1820 and 1847, Uhlhorn steam-powered lever presses were installed at the mints in Germany and also at the Royal Mint. In 1835 a French engineer named Thonnelier invented an improved steam press, which was in use at the Paris and Philadelphia Mints by 1840.

Thereafter, steam presses spread rapidly to the world's mints. Electric power was substituted in the 1880s and presses capable of striking 200 coins a minute, under a pressure of 180 tonnes, were developed during the 20th century. Today the Cincinnati Milacron presses of the Royal Mint and US Mint can strike up to 700 coins a minute.

DIE PRODUCTION
Dies continued to be engraved by hand in the time-honoured fashion until the mid-19th century. Everything still depended on the skill of the engraver, who cut the design directly into the

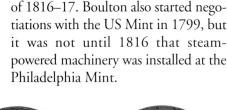

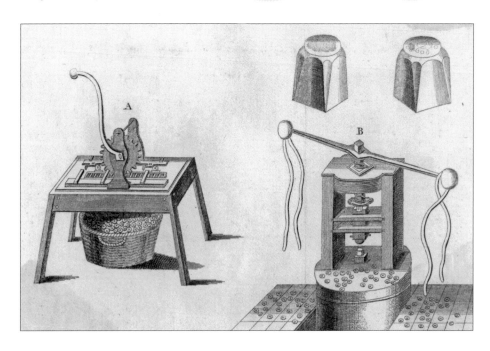

face of the die. The discovery that steel could be chemically hardened, however, meant that it was possible to produce secondary dies, via an intermediate punch called a hub, from the master die. Alternatively, a positive image could be cut in relief on a metal punch and struck into a piece of softer metal, which was then hardened for use as a die. The technique of hubbing appears to have been known in classical times, although no hubs have survived from antiquity. This technique meant that working dies could be rapidly multiplied, greatly accelerating the mass production of coins.

Around 1715, Konstantin Nartov of the Moscow Mint invented a machine that could reduce a large sculpted model to the size required for a coin die. This revolutionized coin production by eliminating the hand engraving previously carried out on the master die, although it has been argued that the change of practice resulted in more stereotyped, less artistic designs.

Improved models were built in Paris between 1757 and 1824, and were applied with varying success to the production of steel dies from large plaster models. Perfected by M. Collas, these

Above: The large-scale plaster model is perfected before the design is reduced to create a hub of the correct size.

Above: The hub is coated with chemicals to harden it so that it can be used to produce a working die.

machines were in regular use at the Paris Mint from then onward, but it was not until 1839 that they were adopted by the Royal Mint; they spread to other European and American mints in the mid-19th century. The process is now carried out by the Contamin portrait lathe and the Janvier die-cutting machine.

FROM WAX MODEL TO FINISHED COIN

The progression from original concept to finished coin involves a number of different skills and processes, and since the 1830s, a series of mechanical processes have replaced the direct engraving of dies. A sculptor makes a wax model at least four times the size of the required coin. A plaster cast is created from the wax model, and from this a nickel-faced copper electrotype is produced. This is placed on the reducing machine, which operates on the pantographic principle. A tracer at one end of the proportional arm moves over the entire surface of the model. At the other end a cutting stylus, like the needle of a record player (but moving from the centre outward) cuts an exact but mathematically reduced reproduction to produce a positive punch, or hub. The hub is chemically hardened and driven into a cone of soft steel to produce the working die. In turn, this is also chemically hardened and is then ready for striking.

CIRCULATING AND PROOF COINS

Today, all coins intended for general circulation are produced on high-speed presses. The blanks are fed into the dial plates and pass through two checking points, which determine that they are of the correct thickness and diameter before they reach the coining station.

Each coin, as it is struck, passes a security counter, which keeps a record of the precise number of coins the machine has struck. The coins are then check-weighed and examined carefully for any flaws. After this examination they are counted again and hermetically sealed in the bags in which they will eventually be distributed to banks.

Proof coins were originally pieces struck to test the dies to ensure perfection before the start of production. They were struck individually by hand, often using specially polished blanks. From this arose the use of proof coins for presentation purposes, but since the mid-19th century they have increasingly been produced expressly for sale to collectors. Today, proof versions of coins are often struck in precious metals, while the circulating versions are in base metals. Although modern proofs are produced by machine like other coins, they are generally struck up to four times, using special dies with frosted relief and polished blanks to provide a sharper contrast between the image and the background.

Hubbing

Using a reducing machine, the enlarged image is transferred to a piece of steel known as the hub, in the precise dimensions of the coin. The next stage, known as hubbing, transfers the positive image from the hub to the working die, which is the negative image used to strike the coins.

SPECIAL PRODUCTION TECHNIQUES

Proof coins, intended not for general circulation but for collectors, are not only struck to a much higher standard than circulating coins, but are usually produced in precious metals and consequently sold at a much higher price than ordinary coins. In recent years many special techniques have evolved, which have revolutionized the production of coins intended for the numismatic market. These include the addition of coloured finishes, precious stones and even holographic designs.

PROOFS

It is probable that test impressions have been made from coinage dies since the striking of coins began. In the days of direct engraving they were struck for the purpose of checking details of the positive image, such as ensuring that the lettering was the right way round. Proofs were often pulled on blanks made of lead or some very soft alloy, which enabled the details to be more clearly seen. From this arose the custom of striking proofs in metals other than those that were to be used for the issued coins – variations now termed

Below: Working mints keep a large stock of coin blanks for striking proofs. These are handled with great care.

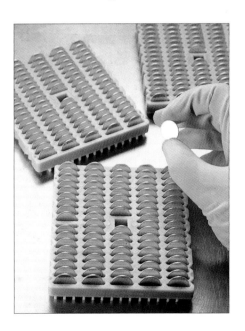

Jewel-Studded Coins

A very recent development has been the incorporation of precious stones in the surface of a coin to create a jewelled effect. One of the first coins of this type celebrated the centenary of the Diamond Jubilee of Queen Victoria, appropriately with a diamond inset.

"off-metal strikes". Nowadays, coins issued in base metals, such as cupro-nickel, are often struck as proofs in silver or even platinum, while gold is sometimes used for proofs of coins normally circulating in brass.

What was a widespread minting tradition has now become an important aspect of the numismatic business, as proofs are prepared specially for the collector. Proofs of this type were first marketed in the middle of the 19th century, the US Mint producing such sets for sale from 1858 onward. Royal Mint proof sets had first been produced in 1826 as presentation issues for a privileged few (such as members of the royal family and senior government officials), but in Britain proof sets sold to the public date from the golden jubilee of Queen Victoria in 1887.

The practice of issuing proofs has now reached the point at which many modern sets exist only in proof form and are not backed by any circulating coins. Modern proofs and deluxe versions of coins are struck on special

Above: A gilt copper proof 2 reas of the East India Company, produced in 1794.

slow-speed presses, in which each piece is struck up to four times to bring up the fine detail. The blanks are specially polished with mops made of linen, calico and swansdown to produce the "mirror table" effect, and the dies are often specially engraved so that the high points have a frosted relief that contrasts with the mirror-like surface.

Until not so long ago it was the norm for blanks to be prepared to produce an overall polished appearance. This is still employed but is often relegated to a version of the base-metal coins sold to the public under such descriptions as "specimen", "library finish" or "special select". These, with a better finish than the circulating coins, are usually marketed in special folders, whereas proofs may be contained in leatherette cases with a velvet lining.

The Franklin Mint (1975–77) frequently offered coin sets in three distinct versions, classified as "matte", "special uncirculated" and "proof". The Pobjoy Mint devised the terms "Proof 4" (proof coins struck four times), "BU2" (brilliant uncirculated struck twice) and "diamond finish" for base metal coins in a finish superior to the general circulating coins.

PATTERNS

In many cases, when a new coin is being considered, the authorities will commission several trial designs, developed all the way to actual production, so that the coinage committee can examine actual pieces before making their decision. Those pieces that are

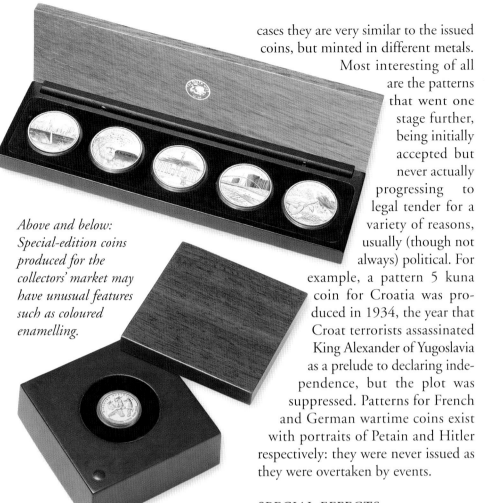

Above and below: Special-edition coins produced for the collectors' market may have unusual features such as coloured enamelling.

rejected and not put into production are known as patterns. Patterns may also arise if the design has been altered or modified in some way before going into production. Patterns of this type are often uniface or bear words such as "Specimen", "Trial", "Prova", "Prueba" or "Probe" (which actually signify "test" in other languages). Many mints, when tendering for a contract, would prepare sample coins to demonstrate design. If the contract were eventually awarded to a competing mint, these samples would be regarded as patterns.

The numismatic appeal of patterns is partly psychological; the rejected design often seems superior to the accepted one because the latter is debased by familiarity. On the other hand, though many patterns have been rejected because they were judged to be impractical as actual coins, they are beautiful works of art. Patterns have a special appeal to collectors as examples of what might have been. In many cases they are very similar to the issued coins, but minted in different metals. Most interesting of all are the patterns that went one stage further, being initially accepted but never actually progressing to legal tender for a variety of reasons, usually (though not always) political. For example, a pattern 5 kuna coin for Croatia was produced in 1934, the year that Croat terrorists assassinated King Alexander of Yugoslavia as a prelude to declaring independence, but the plot was suppressed. Patterns for French and German wartime coins exist with portraits of Petain and Hitler respectively: they were never issued as they were overtaken by events.

SPECIAL EFFECTS

Most modern coins have the design and inscription standing out in relief, but from time to time "intaglio" images occur, which appear as if cut into the surface, and an inscription may be "incuse" (cut into a raised surround). Incuse lettering on raised rims was a distinctive feature of the British Cartwheel copper coins of 1797, while the USA issued gold quarter and half eagles (1908–29) in which the Indian head (obverse) and eagle (reverse) were intaglio. Unfortunately such coins tended to accumulate grime in circulation and ended up looking rather dirty. The technique was revived by the Royal Mint for the 20 pence coin in 1982, but in this case only the inscriptions are incuse.

Raised edges with incuse inscriptions have been used to startling effect by the Pobjoy Mint since the 1980s. This private mint has been at the cutting edge of minting technology for many years and has pioneered the use of special surfaces. In 1990, for example, the crown coins celebrating the 150th anniversary of the Penny Black stamp had a black surface: the technique remains a closely guarded secret but the coin won the coveted Coin of the Year Award. Subsequent issues, appropriately coloured, have reproduced other famous stamps, such as the Blue Mauritius and the Black on Magenta 1 cent of British Guiana. The Pobjoy Mint has also, in recent years, led the way in the development of coins with holographic surfaces.

The Royal Canadian Mint pioneered coins in silver with a small motif inset in gold, used effectively in a series tracing the development of aviation, with portraits of aviators in gold. This technique has since been copied by other mints, notably Pobjoy, which took it a step further with insets of diamonds and other precious stones. Several mints, notably the Singapore Mint, have produced coins with latent images that change, like a hologram, as the surface is tilted.

While the enamelling of existing coins, to transform them into jewels for watch chains, earrings or brooches, has been practised for centuries, a number of special issues are now actually produced with multicoloured surfaces. The effect is usually achieved by adapting silk-screen and lithographic processes to this very exacting medium.

Below: The reverse of the silver crown celebrating the 150th anniversary of the Penny Black, the world's first adhesive postage stamp, in 1990. The surface was specially treated to produce an image of the stamp in black.

COMBATING THE COUNTERFEITER

For as long as coins have existed, there have been attempts to forge them, undermining public confidence as well as losing revenue for the issuing authority. The term "counterfeit" is derived from the French word for imitation and applies to copies of coins (and banknotes) that are intended to deceive and defraud people.

Throughout coin-producing history, strenuous efforts have always been made to deter counterfeiters, by threat of severe punishment as well as by making coins very difficult to imitate.

DEBASEMENT

Counterfeiting may not be the world's oldest profession but it has certainly existed as long as coinage itself: coin hoards dating from the 6th century BC have been found to include staters of Aegina with a copper core and a silver wash, passed off as genuine silver coins. There is even a case of official counterfeits, such as the lead pieces covered with gold, which Polykrates of Samos (532–21 BC) is said to have used to buy off the Spartans.

In the classical and medieval periods counterfeiting occurred frequently and was particularly prevalent in the Middle

Below: A clipped groat of Richard III (top) and clipped shilling of Charles I (bottom). The latter circulated until 1694, when they were finally demonetized and melted down.

Ages, when genuine coins were often poorly struck. The fact that many governments deliberately debased their coinage from time to time did not help.

The most blatant examples were the "crockards" and "pollards" manufactured by many petty lordships in Europe, which copied highly prized English sterling pennies. They flooded England in the 13th century, and when all attempts by Edward I to suppress them failed he made a virtue of necessity by legitimizing them and allowing them to pass current as halfpence. As the imitations contained more than a halfpennyworth of silver, this was a pretty shrewd decision. As a result, the crockards rapidly vanished, although they were not actually demonetized and declared illegal until 1310. This did not prevent a recurrence in the reign of Edward III (1327–77), when England was flooded with base coins known as "lushbournes" (a corruption of the name Luxembourg, whence they came).

CLIPPING COINS

Another age-old method of counterfeiting involved the slicing off of tiny slivers of gold or silver from the edges of coins. The edges were then filed down to give the appearance of normality. Sometimes forgers produced imitation gold and silver coins from base metals, but more often they bought clippings and melted them down to produce counterfeits with a reasonable proportion of precious metal, alloyed with copper.

COUNTER MEASURES

The major breakthrough against counterfeiting came with the widespread adoption of milled coins in Europe during the 17th century. This made it possible to employ sophisticated techniques to improve the appearance of coins generally, making it harder to produce accurate copies. The minting process also used specific methods to stamp out dishonest coining practices.

Above: The trials carried out by the Pyx office of the Royal Mint, London, were instrumental in distinguishing legitimate coins from copies.

SECRET MARKINGS

Various marks have been used to defeat the forger. Medieval English coins had tiny symbols, known as mint-marks, which appeared at the beginning of the inscription and denoted the period between Trials of the Pyx (the periodic assaying of coins at Goldsmiths Hall to test the gold and silver, named from the chest the coins were carried in). In more recent times mint-marks have identified the place where coins were struck and either appear as initials or tiny symbols in various parts of the design.

Privy or secret marks are intended for security purposes and include die numbers or letters engraved microscopically. In some cases privy marks have been used to transform definitives into commemorative coins, such as the baby's crib on Manx coins that greeted the birth of Prince William in 1982.

SECURITY EDGES

The milling process allowed the use of a specially engraved collar to impress an inscription on the edges of coins.

Counterfeit Coins Today

It has been estimated that more than 1 per cent of the pound coins circulating in Britain are counterfeits. They are easy to detect as even newly forged coins do not "ring true" when bounced on a table. Most lose their brightness very quickly and quite often the edge inscription does not match the reverse motif. Here, the tarnished English arms (left) are the reverse of a forgery, whereas the Welsh motif is the genuine article.

The milled coins that went into general circulation in Britain in 1662 bore a Latin motto around the edge – "Decus et Tutamen" ("An ornament and a safeguard") followed by "Anno Regni" ("in the year of the reign") and a date in Roman numerals. This effectively stamped out the practice of clipping. Many countries have resorted to edge inscriptions of this kind as a security feature. The lettering may be either raised or incuse, and often includes tiny ornamental flourishes.

Below: Today, subtle security inscriptions are incorporated into the designs of all coins to foil counterfeiters.

GRAINING

The most common form of safeguard against the clipping of coins is a pattern of fine grooves running across the edge, at right angles to the rim. In common parlance this is often referred to as "milling", but this is a misnomer.

The grain on British and American coins usually consists of fine vertical serrations, but some coins have been produced at various times with a coarser or finer grain, and having to count the number of notches threatens the advanced numismatist with a nasty headache and crossed eyes!

An interrupted grain may be found on some coins, with sections of vertical grooves alternating with plain sections. Its purpose is to assist partially sighted and blind people in distinguishing between coins of high and low value. In some countries graining takes the form of short lines set at an angle, and this is known as a cable edge. When Britain adopted pound coins in 1982 both graining and an incuse edge inscription were used.

PENALTIES

The treatment of counterfeiters has varied over the centuries and from country to country. Forgery was frequently a capital offence, and very special gruesome punishments were reserved for this crime. In England forgers were usually hanged, but the forgery of coins by women seems to have been regarded as particularly heinous, for several female counterfeiters were publicly burned at the stake as late as 1789. Boiling in oil was the preferred punishment in Germany, while in France it was breaking on a wheel; beheading was a common punishment elsewhere. In Russia counterfeiters had molten lead poured down their throats. First offenders were sometimes dealt with more leniently, merely losing a hand or an eye.

In Britain, the Coinage Offences Act of 1861 set out a series of penalties ranging from two years' imprisonment to penal servitude for life. The more severe penalties were meted out for

Above: The practice of graining or inscribing the edges of coins, to mark them as genuine, continues today.

counterfeiting gold or silver coins. Lesser offences included the gilding of farthings and sixpences to pass them off as half sovereigns, the possession of moulds, machines and tools clandestinely removed from the Royal Mint, and the impairment or diminution of gold and silver coins by filing or clipping (or even the possession of such filings and clippings). The Coinage Act of 1870 made provision for the counterfeiting of base metal coins of any kind. Today, US law dictates that counterfeiting is a felony, punishable by a large fine and a maximum of ten years' imprisonment.

Below: The arrest of a pair of coin counterfeiters in the early 19th century.

HISTORY OF PORTRAITURE

We talk about "heads" and "tails" to denote the obverse and reverse of coins. The former nickname derives from the fact that it is the side often reserved for the most important aspect of the coin, the effigy of the head of state.

By the time of the Hellenistic kingdoms, portraiture on coins was exceedingly lifelike. It attained its peak during the Roman Empire, but the Romans rarely attempted a facing portrait – something that modern mints attempt occasionally, but seldom with any real success. The full-face portraits on Byzantine coins tended to become stereotyped, and the full-face portraits on European medieval coins were very crude and undoubtedly symbolic rather than true likenesses.

During the Renaissance the large silver coins of Italy revived the art of portraiture. Modern portrait coins are still predominantly generated by the age-old method of sculpting a profile; photo-engraving has also been used in many instances, though the results are invariably much flatter.

EARLY PORTRAITS

There are examples of coins from the 6th century BC that show a human effigy, such as the head of a warrior (Ephesus), the head of a discus thrower (Cyzicus, c. 520 BC) and a helmeted profile (Kalymna), but it is not known whether these represented real people.

Below right: The Persian satrap Tissaphernes was the first ruler to appear on a coin, in 411 BC.

Below: Head of Apollo on a coin of the 4th century BC.

The earliest coins bearing identifiable portraits came from the Greek cities. Aphrodite and Athena were followed by Herakles, Zeus and a whole host of deities and heroes, but it was left to Persia to depict the first living person, Darius the Great (521–485 BC), on the gold daric and silver siglos. The figure appears as an archer and remained unchanged for 200 years, but is identifiable as Darius because he wears the spiked crown or *orthe* of the Persian ruler. Coins of Abdera (c. 425 BC) bear a profile identified by the inscription as Pythagoras, who flourished a century earlier, but the first coin to bear a close-up portrait of a living person was the silver tetradrachm of Miletus (411 BC) with the Persian satrap Tissaphernes.

After the death of Alexander the Great his generals carved up the empire into separate kingdoms and his profile began to appear on their coins. The horn of Ammon sprouting from Alexander's temple signified that he had now become a god. This established a precedent, and subsequent rulers of the Hellenistic kingdoms began portraying

Above: The Roman rulers Philip I (244–9, left) and Galerius (305–11, right) featured their wives on coins.

themselves. The notion spread to Rome in the late-Republican period, and Pompey the Great and Julius Caesar were thus honoured. Portraiture flourished in the Roman Empire, featuring not only the emperor but his wife and children, creating a veritable portrait gallery renowned for its realism.

Medieval coins were very crude by comparison, with stylized portraits of rulers on the verge of parody. Most were full-face portraits but they seldom bore any resemblance to the living ruler. There are rare instances of queens being mentioned, though not actually depicted, including Cynefryth, wife of Offa of Mercia (757–96) and Adelaide, wife of Emperor Otto (931).

REVIVAL IN THE WEST

The Byzantine Empire was indirectly responsible for the revival of realistic portraiture on the coins of Western Europe. Shortly before Constantinople fell to the Turks in 1453, Emperor John Palaeologus paid a state visit to Italy, an occasion commemorated by a handsome bronze medal. This triggered a fashion for large portrait medals in Renaissance Italy, which spread to other countries and also inspired the production of coins by the Italian city states. These relatively large coins came to be known as testone (from Italian *testa*, a head), and from this come the English words "testoon" and "tester", once synonymous with "shilling". In England the first testoon, of 1504, bore the first realistic profile of Henry VII, engraved by Alexander Brugsal, but it

Above: This full-face portrait on a Henry VIII testoon is a good likeness of the king. The testoon provided a good medium for larger portraits.

was not until 1544 that the stereotyped full-face portrait disappeared from the penny. Henry VIII adopted a full-face portrait and when he debased the silver content in his shillings the silver wore off the highest point – his nose – hence the nickname Coppernose given to these coins.

DIFFERENT STYLES

Since the revival of realistic portraiture in the 15th century most images have been profiles. In many monarchies, notably Britain, the custom developed of showing alternate rulers facing left or right. (Both George V and George VI faced left, because Edward VIII – whose coins were never issued – would have faced right.) Two or more facing portraits were fashionable in Byzantine coinage and this treatment is also found on many of the multiple thalers of the German states. The most spectacular examples were the Achtbruderthalers of Brunswick, which had side-by-side facing portraits of eight brothers, hence the name.

Vis-à-vis, or face-to-face, portraits have occasionally appeared. They include some Roman imperial coins, notably those of Septimius Severus.

Below: Successive British monarchs, Edward VII (left) and George V (right), facing alternately left and right.

Above: A multiple thaler of Friedrich I, Duke of Saxe-Gotha-Altenburg, of 1690, with seven busts in roundels.

The style was adopted by English coins showing Mary Tudor and Philip II of Spain, and Scottish coins showing Mary Queen of Scots and her first two husbands, either Francis II of France or Henry, Lord Darnley. A crown from the Turks and Caicos Islands (1976) has confrontational portraits of George III and George Washington, and the style was also used for coins marking the wedding of Prince Charles and Lady Diana Spencer in 1981.

Most coins that have two portraits show them as overlapping profiles, with the more important person (such as a king) at the front and the lesser profile behind. These are described as "jugate", "accolated" or "conjoined" profiles, and they have been in use since the gold staters of the Brutii (282 BC). In Britain the style was used for coins of William III and Mary II (1689–94), those of 1981, 1986, 2000 and 2005 celebrating British royal marriages and the Golden Wedding coins of 1997.

The strangest portrait coin of all time must be the Zurich thaler of 1512, with full-face standing portraits of the three martyred saints, Regulus, Exuperant and Felix, beheaded and holding their heads in their hands.

PORTRAITS OF PERSONALITES

The depiction of royalty other than the reigning monarch was popular during the Roman Empire, when relatives of

Right: Triple conjoined portraits of Carol I, Ferdinand and Carol II on a Romanian 20 lei of the latter (1944).

the emperor were often portrayed. The practice was revived in 16th-century Italy, when the large silver coins that were being produced afforded scope for it, but the portraits were still confined to royalty.

Bavaria appears to have produced the first coins commemorating historic personalities other than royalty, beginning with the thaler of 1826 mourning the deaths of the engineer Georg Friedrich von Reichenbach (1772–1826) and the physicist Joseph von Fraunhofer (1787–1826), whose face-to-face profiles appear on the reverse. Several Bavarian coins of 1840–9 depicted the statues of famous men from Albrecht Dürer to Orlando di Lasso. This notion was not copied elsewhere until 1893, when the USA struck a half dollar portraying Christopher Columbus (followed by many other similar coins) and Brazil similarly honoured Pedro Cabral in 1900.

Below: Personalities featured on recent coins include (clockwise from top left) sporting heroes (Roger Bannister, Britain), poets (Robert Burns, Isle of Man), explorers (Captain Cook, New Zealand) and royalty (Charles and Diana's engagement, New Zealand).

NON-FIGURAL MOTIFS

After their adoption of Islam as the prominent faith in the 7th century, Arab countries did not place any effigy of a living creature, either man or beast, on their coins. Although the portrayal of animate objects was considered to be closely linked to idolatry, and was thus declared taboo by the teachings of the Koran, there was no such ban on the depiction of inanimate objects. Nevertheless, until the middle of the 20th century, Islamic coins continued to be devoid of either portraits or pictures, and the space on both sides of the coins was entirely given over to inscriptions in Arabic. This restraint created a need to be innovative with the use of text, leading to some of the lengthiest – and most poetic – inscriptions ever to appear on coins anywhere in the world.

Above: The fusion of Persian and Arab styles has resulted in a few ancient examples of portraiture. This coin depicts Mus'ab bin al-Zubayr.

Below: Abbasid coins usually have the name of the current ruler's heir on the reverse. The bottom example is unusual for bearing the name of an unborn heir.

PIOUS INVOCATIONS

Not only did the countries that produced these coins develop increasingly ornate styles of script, but the inscriptions themselves became more flowery as time passed. The standard formula that appears on Islamic coins is known as the Bismillah, and is the first word of the affirmation, "There is no God but God, and Muhammad is His Prophet." By tradition Allah had 99 excellent names, but opinions differ as to what those 99 names were. In fact, no fewer than 132 epithets for Allah are recorded on Islamic coins. They range from the simple "The One" to "The Ever Self-existing One". Other versions found in inscriptions include "He Who Hath Not Been Begotten", "The Very Next Adjoining One" or the more prosaic "The Numberer" and "The Road Guide".

Muslims had no monopoly on the name of God by any means, but what made their coins so special was their purity of design: they were not sullied by portraits or images of animals or anything else that might distract the thoughts of the faithful.

WIDESPREAD USE OF ARABIC

Arabic was widely used, not only in Arabia and the lands conquered by the Arabs, from Spain to Mesopotamia, but also for the Farsi inscriptions on the coins of Persia and Afghanistan, and for the Malay texts on coins of Java, Sumatra and Malaya. Arabic was the script used by the Mughal emperors, the princely states and even the Honourable East India Company. On some coins of the Indian states Queen Victoria was named (though she was not portrayed) and styled in Arabic as Empress of India.

The earliest Islamic coins combined Arabic with Graeco-Roman or Sasanian (Pehlevi) inscriptions. Siculo-Norman coins were copied from Ayyubid coins but with a Christian formula in Arabic, "Victorious by the Grace of God" on

Above: Ornate punches replaced effigies on some post-Gupta Indian coins. The lotus motif is a good example of the use of recognized emblems.

Above: Zubayda, the wife of the Abbasid governor Al-Rashid, was perhaps the first woman to strike a coin in the history of Islam. The inscription reads: "By the command of the lady, mother of the heir apparent, may God preserve her, so be it."

gold taris of Tancred. Alfonso VIII of Castile struck coins inscribed in Arabic, "Amir of the Catholics and the Pope the Imam of the Church of the Messiah".

For the purposes of trade with Muslim merchants in Morocco, Portuguese copper ceitils were struck with a three-line Arabic inscription bearing the name and title of King Manuel I (1495–1521).

TITLES

Islamic coins bore the names and titles of rulers, and Abbasid coins often mentioned the heir to the throne as well – even if the heir was as yet unborn and unnamed. Titles, although extravagant and self-aggrandizing, were also carefully worded to underline religious commitment and the earthly confines of the territories over which a ruler presided. They included "Excellent King of the Surface of the Earth" (used by the Mongol rulers of Persia),

Sun Motif

While some coins of Hyderabad depicted the Char Minar gateway, its feudatory dependency of Indore struck coins with a smiling sun motif, the nearest thing to a portrait without actually being one.

"Emperor of the World" (for the Jahandar of Delhi) and "Lord of the World" (for the Atabeg of Mosul). By contrast, the most self-abasing title of all time was inscribed on Islamic coins, Shah Tahmasp I of Persia (1514–76) being content to refer to himself as "Slave of Ali". Not to be outdone, Shah Rukh was styled "Hound of the Threshold of the Pleasing One" and his successor, Shah Husain, went a step further with "Hound of the Threshold of Ali, of the Amir of the Faithful".

The most charming title found in an Islamic inscription was that favoured by some of the Indian princely states in the 19th century, after the proclamation of the Empire of India in 1877: "Queen Victoria, Adorning the Throne of Inglistan [England] and Hind". The saddest title was "Deceased", inscribed in Arabic on the coins of Aziz Sheikh of the Golden Horde and Tipu Sultan, ruler of Mysore, which were issued shortly after their deaths.

SIGN OF THE TOUGHRA

The *toughra* found on Turkish and Arab coins is the Islamic counterpart of the royal monogram on European coins. It consists of an elaborate Arabic inscription giving the names of a ruler and his father and incorporating three vertical lines. These date from the reign of Sultan Murad I (1359–89), who, when signing important documents, dipped three fingers into the inkwell and drew them down the page.

CHRONOGRAMS

A chronogram is an inscription in which some letters can be read as Roman numerals, which make a date when added together. (The term is derived from the Greek and means "time writing".)

This unusual practice was popular in Europe in the Renaissance and the 17th century, when it was often used to signify dates in inscriptions on tombstones and foundation stones, but it was derived from the Arab custom of giving the letters of the *abjad* (the Arabic alphabet) a numerical value. From this came the fashion for concealing the date in inscriptions on Islamic coins, which could be deduced by adding up the value of the letters composing the word or words.

Thus, coins inscribed in the name of the ruler Fakhr al-Din Qara Arslan, Artuqid of Hisn Kayfa, contained a final word whose letters signified 500, 50 and 6, making the date 556 AH. On the reverse of coins of Nadir Shah appeared the inscription, "By the Tarikh, Whatever Happens is Best." The letters of this phrase as written in Arabic had the values 70 + 100 + 6 + 1 + 40 + 10 + 80 + 200 + 10 + 600 + 30 + 1, which together made 1148 AH.

A mohur of Jahangir bears the inscription: "The letters of Jahangir and Allahu Akbar's are Equal in Value from the Beginning of Time", and, indeed, when added up the letters of their names each total 289.

Below: The toughra is a feature of Ottoman coins (top) and Islamic coins of the Indian princely states (bottom); Egypt included an actual portrait of King Fu'ad I in 1921, and Morocco worked the national star emblem into an ornate reverse of 1900.

Below: Ancient Islamic coiners sought innovative ways of displaying their lengthy inscriptions, from hexagonal, circular and star-shaped arrangements to densely packed central legends.

HISTORY OF PICTORIALISM

The obverse of a coin was traditionally reserved for the portrait of a deity or ruler, while the reverse (the "tails") was used for an image of lesser importance. The distinction has been blurred in more recent times by the adoption of arms instead of a portrait (especially in republics) or, conversely, the use of portraiture on both sides.

Because of the symbolic importance of coins, pictorial elements often arise out of armorial emblems and they, in turn, may be traced back to mythology. The use of animals (particularly cattle and horses) may symbolize power and wealth. From the 1900s onward, as coins in general have become more pictorial, they have often illustrated national aspirations. By the 1930s a didactic or propaganda element was creeping in, particularly on coins of the USSR and fascist countries.

CLASSICAL IMAGES

The simple motifs on the obverse of the earliest electrum dumps probably represented the personal badges of the merchants and magistrates who authorized them. In the heyday of classical Greek coinage the civic emblem was the dominant feature of many issues. Among the earliest examples were the

Below: Motifs on ancient Greek and Persian coins include ordinary animals as well as mythical creatures such as a winged Pegasus or Gorgon.

winged boar (Klazomenai), boar (Methymna), calves' heads (Lesbos), lion's head (Lindos), amphora (Andros), frog (Seriphos), dolphins (Thera) and bull's head (Athens). Some of the emblems were a pun on the name of the city or district. Thus the *bous* or cowhide shield graced the coins of Boeotia, while a crab and a turtle were featured on the coins of Akragas and Aegina respectively. Others featured mythical figures associated with the area, such as the boy Taras riding a dolphin (Tarentum) and Athena with her owl (Athens).

Heraldic reverses related to portrait obverses developed in the 5th century BC, and from matching deities with their familiars, such as Zeus and the eagle, it was but a short step to the coins of imperial Rome, with the emperor on one side and an allegorical subject on the other. The Romans, however, eventually produced coins that had a wide range of subjects on the reverse, including the famous buildings and landmarks of the Roman Empire. It is on some of these that we find the earliest representation of the original Tower of London.

MEDIEVAL DEPICTIONS

Most medieval coins tended to show the stylized portrait of a ruler on the obverse and a cross on the reverse, partly out of Christian sentiment but also partly for the practical purpose of showing where the coin could be cut into halves or quarters. The revival of

Below: Favoured motifs for Roman coins included a standing bull (left) or landmarks such as the Temple of Jupiter (right).

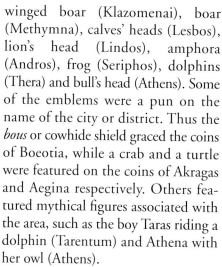

Above and left: Dionysus, god of wine, is often depicted on ancient Greek coins of Thrace, the site of his sanctuary.

symbolism came in the early 10th century when Pope Benedict I sanctioned denarii whose reverse showed an open hand flanked by the letters R and O. The hand (*manus* in Latin) was a pictogram substituting for part of the word "Romanus". The hand of God raised in benediction was a popular theme on coins, especially as the dreaded millennium approached and people feared the end of the world. Extremely rare pennies of Aethelred the Unready had an obverse of the Lamb of God and reverse of a dove, and are believed to allude to the millennium.

Heraldic reverses were adopted by the Frankish rulers. Early coins had a stylized temple, but with the growth of chivalry in the 12th and 13th centuries it became fashionable to place the emblem from the ruler's escutcheon on the reverse. Thus began the convention, prevalent on many coins to this day, of having the ruler's portrait on the obverse and the national arms on the reverse. English gold coins may be found with the Archangel Michael slaying the serpent or the monarch armed and standing in a galleon, but it was not until the neo-classical Britannia (1797) and St George and the Dragon (1816) that pictorialism truly emerged.

MODERN PICTORIALS

In classical times, coins could be startlingly graphic in the subjects they featured. Drunkenness, rape and debauchery appeared on Greek

Above: A "death thaler" of the ruler August II of Saxony, showing a skull lying at the base of a tree.

staters from Thasos (Thrace) and Lete and tetradrachms of Mende and Naxos, reflecting a very earthy approach to subjects considered taboo in later times. Pictorialism as such, however, really began with the large thalers and guldengroschen from the 16th century. Their modern counterparts, dollars and crowns, offer considerable scope for elaborate pictorial motifs.

The large silver coins of the German states tended to be allegorical or propagandistic, particularly during the Thirty Years War (1618–48). Republican France's first pictorial coin, the 5 décime piece of 1793, was in the same genre. Popularly known as the Robespierre décime, its elaborate obverse depicts Nature as an Egyptian goddess expressing the water of life from her breasts. Robespierre (the President of the Convention) is offering a cup of the fluid to a delegate of the Assembly.

Austria and the German states took the lead in developing pictorial coins in the 19th century; the earliest issues

to depict ships and locomotives come from that area. But it was in the course of the 20th century that pictorial coins really came into their own. Pictorialism was no longer confined to large commemorative pieces but extended right down to the lowliest definitive circulating coins. The Irish Free State (later the Republic of Ireland) adopted distinctive coins in 1928 and these bore reverse motifs showing such subjects as a sow and piglets (halfpenny), a hen and chickens, a hare (3 pence), a hound (6 pence) and a bull (shilling). The Barnyard series, as it was nicknamed, continued for many years, surviving until 1968. Canada, Australia and New Zealand adopted pictorial motifs in the 1930s, while Britain introduced a series in 1937 depicting a wren (farthing), Sir Francis Drake's ship (halfpenny) and a clump of sea thrift (3 pence); other denominations retained the seated figure of Britannia (penny) or clung to heraldic themes.

Beginning with Lincoln in 1909 (the centenary of his birth), American coins have favoured portraits of dead presidents (obverse) and buildings associated with them, such as the Lincoln Memorial (1 cent) and Monticello, the home of Thomas Jefferson (5 cents), but otherwise heraldic and symbolic motifs predominate. The only truly pictorial United States coin was the

Below: Coins of the Weimar Republic depicting Cologne Cathedral (top) and a scenic river reverse to mark the liberation of the Rhineland.

nickel of 1913–38, which had the head of a Native American on the obverse and a buffalo on the reverse. In 2005 these much-loved motifs were revived after a gap of 67 years.

Pictorialism today is prominent in the coins of the emerging nations, but examples are also found in Scandinavia and Britain's crown dependencies. For Greece, Italy and Israel the wheel has come full circle, with heavy reliance on classical or biblical pictorial motifs.

Below: A naval obverse of Virginia (top) and a mountain lion reverse of Vermont are just two of the pictorial subjects used on American commemorative issues.

HOW TO COLLECT

Numismatics boasts distinguished enthusiasts, many of whom used the hobby to develop a keen interest in history. Once you have decided on a focus for your collection, you can begin to make new acquisitions. Although it's tempting to seek out rarities, many issues of recent years – such as this enamelled coin of the Isle of Man – are truly resplendent.

ORIGINS OF NUMISMATICS

Numismatics is the name given to the study and collecting of coins and medals, and is derived from *nomisma*, the Greek word for coin. It is probable that coins were prized for their aesthetic qualities from the earliest times, while their importance in socio-economic development was appreciated by Herodotus and other early historians.

There were certainly coin collections during the earliest times – but not, perhaps, in the modern sense. In the era before banking existed, people stored their surplus wealth in leather bags or in earthenware jars, which could be buried in troubled times. Most hoards were presumably retrieved by their owners when the crisis passed, but many others were never recovered until turned up by the plough or (more likely nowadays) discovered by the

Above: Great royal coin collectors include (clockwise from top left) Carol I of Romania, Christina of Sweden, Habsburg Emperor Charles VI and Prince Rainier of Monaco.

Right: Chocolate replica of the 1 euro coin, produced in 2000 to publicize the new currency.

Below: Chinese gold panda coin, distributed as a Lunar New Year gift in a red silk purse.

metal detector. Coins from such hoards, large and small, have long held a fascination for the archaeologist and antiquary, and they are undoubtedly the source of much of the material now in the hands of museums and some collectors. Unfortunately, until relatively recently, such hoards were not carefully preserved and studied scientifically, although laws now exist in some countries to safeguard archaeological finds, including those of numismatic interest, until they can be properly catalogued by the appropriate authority.

EARLIEST COIN CATALOGUES
Although St Thomas Aquinas (1225–74) touched on coinage in his philosophical writings, the earliest works dealing with numismatics, or the antiquarian aspects of coins, as opposed

to the monetary and financial aspects of current coins, appeared early in the 16th century. The French antiquary Guillaume Budé (1467–1540) published *De Asse et Partibus Eius* ("Concerning the Roman As and its Parts") and *Libellus de Moneta Graeca* ("A Pamphlet of Greek coins").

Many other books appeared in the 17th and 18th centuries, in France, Germany and Italy, dealing with various aspects of ancient and medieval coins. By the early 19th century, the practice of coin-collecting was well enough established to support periodical literature. The earliest magazine devoted to numismatics was *Blätter für Münzkunde*, published in Hanover from 1834 until 1844 by Dr Hermann Grote. *The Numismatic Chronicle*, founded by John Young Ackerman, made its debut as a quarterly in 1836 and is still going strong as the journal of the Royal Numismatic Society.

The second half of the 19th century witnessed the publication of a profusion of catalogues and handbooks, consisting of either systematic listings of coins in the world's major public collections or studies of particular regions and periods, predominantly Greek and Roman but with a developing interest in medieval European and Islamic coins. From the tone and contents of these early works it is clear that the emphasis was on ancient coins, which collectors who had had the benefit of a classical education could appreciate.

Numismatics continued to be predominantly classical in character until the late 19th century. By that time, some wealthy collectors in North America were taking a keen interest in

Royal Collector

Victor Emanuel III of Italy (1900–46) succeeded to the throne on the assassination of his father, and by his own abdication hastened the end of the Italian monarchy. Today he is best remembered for his magnificent coin collection, now in the Palazzo Massimo alle Terme, Rome.

the coins of the United States, yet the earliest book on the subject was not published until 1899.

Catalogues of the coins of the various European countries began to appear in the 1880s, but a similar coverage of the coins of India, China, Japan, Korea and other Asiatic countries did not develop until the turn of the century. These catalogues varied considerably in detail and illustration. No attempt was made to produce priced catalogues until the 1920s, when such books covering specific countries or periods began to appear regularly. The only catalogues that cover world coinage as a whole are the Krause catalogues, published in the USA (and confined to the modern period).

GREAT COIN COLLECTIONS

From the Renaissance onward, it was fashionable for gentlemen to possess a coin cabinet (which in some cases was an entire room, shelved from floor to ceiling to house their treasures). Outstanding among early collectors were the Italian poet Petrarch, the Medici rulers of Florence, Pope Paul II, Queen Christina of Sweden and the Habsburg Emperor Charles VI. In Britain, King George III set a fine example, and his interest in coins was shared by his personal surgeon, Dr William Hunter (1718–83), whose

wide-ranging collections, including coins and medals, were the nucleus of the Hunterian Museum in Glasgow, opened in 1807. The collections formed by his brother, Dr John Hunter (1728–93), and their contemporary, Sir Hans Soane, formed the basis of the numismatic collections in the British Museum. Britain is unusual in having several great institutional collections, including those in the Ashmolean Museum (Oxford), and the Fitzwilliam Museum (Cambridge), as well as the Royal Scottish Museum (Edinburgh). Elsewhere, large and all-embracing collections are housed in the Bibliothèque Nationale (Paris) and the Smithsonian Institution (Washington).

Among more recent monarchs who had an abiding passion for coins were King Carol of Romania and Prince Rainier of Monaco, but King Victor Emmanuel III of Italy was a lifelong numismatist, whose studies and scholarly writings on the subject are still widely respected. Conversely, King Farouk of Egypt, another royal collector, was really the pack rat par excellence, whose collections ranged from stamps and coins to glass paperweights and ladies' underwear. Some of the greatest collectors of more recent

Above: Promotional sets and souvenir folders are contemporary methods of encouraging budding coin collectors.

times were Americans, such as the pharmaceuticals magnate Eli K. Lilly and the Texan tycoon Nelson Bunker Hunt, who famously tried to corner the world silver market back in the 1970s. The late Mary Norweb was arguably the world's leading female numismatist, and the sale of her incomparable collections in the 1980s was spread over many auctions.

Below: The coin collection of William Hunter (bottom-left), anatomist and surgeon of fellow collector George III (pictured on this 1796 guinea, right), formed the nucleus of Scotland's oldest museum, the Hunterian in Glasgow. The museum, as it was in 1807, is shown in the engraving (bottom right).

GRADE AND CONDITION

Coins are the most durable of all the antiquities and have survived in remarkable condition considering their age. Gold coins have been dug out of the earth gleaming as brightly as the day they were minted. Conversely, modern coins may show rapid signs of wear due to frequent circulation and the rough treatment meted out in slot machines. It follows that the condition of a coin plays a major part in determining its value to a collector.

COIN GRADES

Newcomers to the hobby are often amazed at the enormous disparity in value or price between a coin in impeccable mint condition, with neither scratches on its surface nor irregularities in its edges, and its twin in worn condition. The effigy on the obverse of the latter may have lost its fine detail but surely it is still recognizable? And the coat of arms on the reverse may be reduced to a mere outline, but the date is still readable, so why should it be regarded as worthless?

Everything is relative. Collectors may be quite happy to acquire a medieval coin in generally poor condition because (a) it is a major rarity, or (b) that is the condition of all the known examples of the coin and it would be virtually impossible to find a specimen in a better state. It seems to be the case that, when it comes to medieval

Below: These 18th-century British spade guineas are judged by one auctioneer to be "fair to very fine", though it often takes an expert to discern variations in condition, and reach an overall grading.

Viewing and Assessing Coins

Above: A soft, lint-free cloth offers good protection against surface scratching when setting coins down to view.

Above: A range of magnification tools exist; generally x10 is the maximum strength required to view coins.

Above: If you must handle coins – not recommended for rarities or those in mint state – hold them at the very edges.

Above: Common, circulating coins will arrive in various states, and may be in need of cleaning before viewing closely.

coinage, you will often have to be content with a piece that would otherwise never be considered worthy of a place in your collection. Supply falls far short of demand in this particular area of numismatics. On the other hand, Greek and Roman imperial coins generally exist in such large quantities that their relative condition is a major factor in determining their value.

As for modern coins, anything less than the highest grades of condition should be unacceptable to a collector – a fact that is reflected in the coin catalogues, which usually confine their prices to the two top grades. At the apex of the pyramid, proof coins are collectable only in pristine condition, exactly as they left the mint; anything less makes them unacceptable to the discerning collector.

HOW TO ASSESS GRADE AND CONDITION

The ability to appraise a coin accurately comes only with years of experience. A good magnifier is an absolute necessity, but nowadays you can also scan coins at a high resolution and then view them on screen, focusing on the particular details you wish to examine more closely.

In the highest grade of condition a coin should still possess the original lustre characteristic of a freshly minted coin. Next comes a coin that may have lost some or most of its lustre but on which the finest detail of the design is absolutely sharp. Lower down the scale are coins that show slight evidence of wear on the higher points of the design, such as the hair on the portrait, the fine folds of clothing or the intricate detail

Classification of Condition

Because the conventional terms have tended to become subjective, the American Numismatic Association (ANS) has devised a more scientific and objective system, combining terms or abbreviations with numbers to give a more precise classification. This is now used worldwide by dealers when encapsulating or "slabbing" coins in sealed folders (pictured), to bolster confidence in buying and selling. These grades are as follows:

Proof-70	Perfect proof
Proof-67	Gem proof
Proof-65	Choice proof
Proof-63	Select proof
Proof-60	Proof

Uncirculated coins are graded by Mint State (MS):

MS-70	Perfect
MS-67	Gem
MS-65	Choice
MS-63	Select
MS-60	Uncirculated

The lower grades combine the traditional abbreviations with numbers:

AU-50	About uncirculated
EF-45	Choice extremely fine
EF-40	Extremely fine
VF-30	Choice very fine
VF-20	Very fine
F-12	Fine
VG-8	Very good
G-4	Good
AG-4	About good
BS-1	Basal state

in a coat of arms. Below that, you will notice wear in the inscriptions, with the lettering looking thick or blurred.

Beyond that state, coins showing extensive signs of wear are not worth collecting unless they are very rare. The same is true for coins that bear signs of rough handling – scuff marks, scratches or edge knocks. Coins that have suffered actual damage, such as piercing

Below: Special peel-back holders are available to preserve the condition of individual coins.

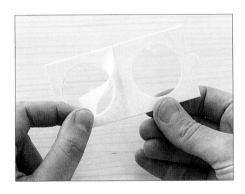

for use as jewellery or clipping to remove slivers of gold or silver from the edges, should be avoided altogether, except as historical curiosities.

NOMENCLATURE

Over the years dealers and collectors have attempted to classify the condition of coins, adopting various terms to define the various states, from "brilliant uncirculated" to the lower grades of "fair", "medium" and "poor". The trouble is that the terms, like the coins themselves, have tended to become worn or debased with the passage of time and as a result new terms have been devised to upgrade the system. At one time, for example, the term "good" meant just that, but nowadays a coin given that epithet would, in fact, be pretty poor and not worth considering unless it was a very elusive item.

Auctioneers and cataloguers should include the quality of the strike with their description. Countermarked coins

will not necessarily lose value if the mark itself is sufficiently clear and complete. Both sides of the coin are assessed during grading: the final evaluation will be based on the slightly weaker of the two sides, if they are not particularly different, or the coin will be given a "split grade" in the catalogue entry. If the two sides are found to be more than one grade apart, this suggests that the design of either the obverse or reverse has been subject to greater wear and tear, and the coin will be graded on the weaker side alone. Coins bearing a small motif, such as a crown symbol, may be graded solely on the condition of this easily worn element of the design. A guide to nomenclature is given with the glossary to this book.

Below: This gold half-anna restrike of an 1892 copper denomination (top left), struck for use in British India, is judged to be in "brilliant" state as it has almost no surface markings. "Peripheral" weakness on the obverse (top right) of a 13th-century issue from Bukhara earns it a split grade of "good/very fine". The "unique" status of these Anglo-Saxon "bonnet-type" pennies (middle) increases value despite their time-worn condition, while this 2 shilling coin of George VI (bottom), sold with its original 1937 proof-set packaging, was graded "about as struck".

LOOKING AFTER COINS

Coins are tough – they have to be in order to carry out their function. For this reason, they have been produced using hard-wearing materials designed to be handled frequently, and to withstand the grime and sweat of hands in every climate and working condition. They have to be robust enough to withstand harsh treatment, such as being shoved into slot machines or dropped on the ground or, worst of all, jostled constantly with other coins in purses and pockets.

PRESERVING CONDITION

Coins are often expected to circulate for decades and, unless there is a change in the currency or a denomination is withdrawn, only when they are too old and worn to be recognizable are they taken out of service. However, even coins bearing the marks of time should be preserved in the condition in which they are found.

Unless you are confining your acquisitions to coins neatly packaged in their pristine state by the mint or numismatic bureau, or slabbed by a dealer of high repute, you will acquire coins in their naked and unadorned state. At best they will have been passed from hand to hand to some extent, even if they are still bright and shiny and bear the current date. At worst they will have been in circulation for some time,

Right: Manage your expectations when caring for your coins. If, for example, they display signs of "copper sickness" such as the coins on the left of this picture, you will never be able to restore them to their original state, like those on the right.

perhaps for many years. They may latterly have reposed in a dealer's oddment tray, the convenient repository for so many unconsidered trifles, waifs and strays, which are too poor or of insufficient value to make it worth the dealer's time and trouble to sort and grade properly. Collectors love sifting through these bargain trays as the cheaper material generally ends up there, where quick turnover is the name of the game.

CLEANING WITH CARE

Once you have borne away your treasures and taken them home for closer examination and identification, before putting them into the appropriate place in your collection the first thing is to attend to their appearance. The plain fact is that most coins that will come into your possession in the ordinary way will be dirty, dull and grimy, even if they still possess some of their original lustre. The oils secreted by human hands, atmospheric pollution and everyday dust and dirt all combine to give circulated coins a fairly unattractive appearance.

Generally speaking, a good degreasing solvent will work wonders in removing surface grime. A drop or two of a good quality lighter fuel on the surface of a coin, gently wiped off with a very soft cloth, will remove all or most of the dirt. For more persistent cases, especially when dirt accumulates in and around the lettering or the more intricate parts of the design, brushing with a soft brush with animal bristles – never use nylon or other artificial fibres – is efficacious.

The watchwords here are gentleness and persistence. It is preferable, when handling coins, to wear latex or fine plastic surgical gloves. If you are not wearing gloves, always hold coins at the very edge, as shown, left, so that any contact between your fingertips and the coin surface is minimal. You would be surprised how indelible fingerprints can be; once a fingerprint marks the surface of a coin, it can never be removed and is etched there for all time.

Cleaning Coins

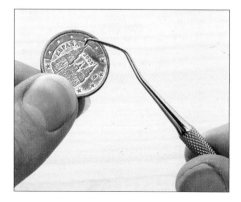

Above: A specially designed coin 'pick' will help to remove encrusted grime.

Above: This coin cleaning brush causes minimal damage to the metal.

SOLUTIONS FOR DIFFERENT METALS

If all coins were made of gold or silver the problems of caring for them would be simple. Gold does not rust, it is impervious to oxidation or atmospheric pollution and it resists most of the chemicals found in the soil. Of course gold coins do get grimy from constant handling, but surface dirt can be easily removed with a solution of lemon juice in an equal amount of warm water. Silver responds well to a bath in warm water to which you have added a few drops of ammonia.

Copper or bronze coins are more of a problem because these metals are prone to oxidation and form the green patina called verdigris. Where this is evenly distributed over the coin, it actually protects the surface from further deterioration, and it is not unattractive in, for example, Roman coins. But where verdigris appears as bright green patches, it is regarded as "copper sickness" and needs special attention. Fortunately, there are now various products on the market that are designed specifically for the cleaning of coins made of different metals. Read the instructions on the label and follow them carefully, and you should be able to cope with this problem.

Below: Basic household items such as an empty jam jar and caustic soda are useful for coin care.

The Perils of Polish

If cleaning should be approached with the utmost caution, polishing is definitely a bad thing! Beginners sometimes fall into the trap of assuming that a vigorous rub with metal cleaner will improve the appearance of a coin, but short of actually hitting it with a hammer and chisel, this is the worst thing you can do. Polishing a coin may briefly improve its superficial appearance, but such abrasive action will destroy the patina and reduce the fineness of the high points of the surface. Even if a coin is polished only once, it will never be the same, and an expert can recognize this immediately.

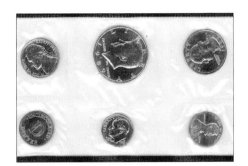

Above: You should never remove coins from any form of sealed packaging unless it is really necessary.

The lower down the electromotive series the metals are, the greater the problem, as these materials have a greater tendency to rust and corrode. This applies particularly to coins minted in times of shortage, such as wartime, which may be made of tin, zinc, iron or steel. In this case, immersion in a 5 per cent solution of caustic soda containing some aluminium foil or zinc filings works well, but care must be taken to rinse the coins thoroughly afterwards in clean water. Cotton buds can be extremely useful accessories for dealing with troublesome patches of dirt or grease. Dry coins carefully with a soft cloth – never use paper towels as these can scratch the metal surface – and always blot coins dry rather than rubbing them.

SALVAGED COINS

Coins recovered from being buried in the ground, or found on the sea bed, may present special problems due to chemical reactions between the metals and the salts present in earth or sea water. Buried silver coins, for example, will acquire a dark patina of silver sulphide. In such cases, the best advice is to take them to your local museum or friendly coin dealer and let the conservation experts decide what can or should be done to improve their condition and appearance.

Left and below: The packaging in which special edition mint sets are issued is designed to preserve the coins into perpetuity.

HOUSING COINS

Like any other collectables of value, coins need to be properly housed. Although they are far less bulky than even small antiques, they are much more cumbersome than stamps or postcards, and have their special requirements in order that they should be kept in a safe and orderly manner. Storage options range from special items of furniture to boxes, cases and albums. Each has its good and bad points, but, in the end, what you use is a matter of personal choice.

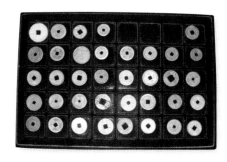

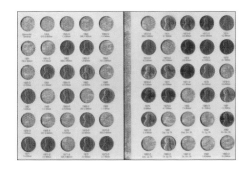

Above: Modern plastic coin trays have a felt lining and compartments, often with a transparent lid and slipcase.

BOXES AND CASES

For those seeking to establish a fairly extensive collection, with room to grow, boxes and cases not only give the "classic" feel of a small library, but are also a useful aid to cataloguing. Companies such as Abafil of Italy and Lindner of Germany produce a large range of cases suitable for coins. They are constructed of steel or stout plastic, and open to reveal several shallow trays, often stacked in such a way that each can be slid in or out of place without disturbing the other trays. The trays themselves have compartments of various dimensions tailored to fit coins of different sizes and are felt lined. Most of these boxes

Above and left: A set of Australian transport tokens in a presentation folder.

have a good locking system and a carrying handle, so they are particularly popular with dealers travelling to and from coin shows. When the case is locked the trays are held securely in place and there is no danger of the coins slithering around or falling out in transit. These cases often have separate

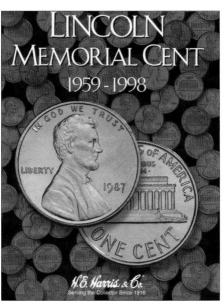

LINCOLN
MEMORIAL CENT
1959-1998

H.E. Harris & Co.
Serving the Collector Since 1916

Above and top: A Harris & Co. Memorial Cent coin folder which, when opened, reveals holes to contain all the variants of a particular denomination, arranged by date and mint-mark.

compartments for such handy accessories as a good magnifier and callipers for accurately measuring diameters and thicknesses. Another useful feature consists of side pockets inside the box for hygroscopic crystals, which ensure that the coins are kept in a dry atmosphere.

The same companies also produce individual cases on the same principle, usually constructed in stout plastic lined with felt, with a sliding plastic lid and a handle. In turn, the case fits inside a slipcase on which you can write the details of the contents. Unlike the boxes, however, these cases seldom have a lock, so they are much less secure. While coin boxes are best simply

Left: There are a number of different ways to house coins, from felt-lined trays to ring-bound albums with clear plastic sleeves, with compartments into which individual coins can be slotted, enabling both sides to be viewed in the sleeve.

stacked on the floor, the cases can be stored on bookshelves – always making sure that you do not overload them. There are also stacking systems that enable you to build up boxes and cases in a single all-purpose storing unit. The German company Mobel-Element, for example, produces a cabinet with a steel frame that can be adapted or added to as your collection grows.

COIN ALBUMS

Stout card coin folders produced by such firms as Harris and Whitman, with holes drilled for different denominations and the date, mint-mark and brief description printed below each hole, have long been immensely popular with American collectors. Similar albums have been produced for coins of other countries. While they are ideal for change-checkers intent on completing all the dates and mint-marks of a particular coin, they lack the flexibility required for a general collection.

In the 1960s, when coin collecting grew dramatically in popularity, a number of stationers began producing coin albums. These had a leatherette binder and a stout steel post with two or four

Below: A souvenir presentation case with a slipcase, housing a set of coins celebrating the Chinese Year of the Dog.

rings on to which transparent pages with pockets of various sizes could be threaded. These albums have the advantage of allowing you to see both sides of the coin merely by turning the page – a big improvement over traditional cabinet trays. If they are stored upright on bookshelves the weight of the coins tends to distort the pages and may even pull the steel post away from the spine, so for this reason they are best laid flat, like coin cases.

WALLETS

Plastic wallets are designed to hold individual coins, and are used in conjunction with larger containers such as albums. They often have a small sleeve into which a card giving details of the coin can be inserted. These wallets have largely superseded traditional manilla envelopes, but both can be stacked upright in narrow cases. You can buy cases for this purpose that build into storage systems, but many collectors are content to use any long, narrow box. Today many mints issue coin sets in special folders or wallets, and these can be stored in the compartments of coin cases, or slotted into albums.

CABINETS

Wealthy collectors of former times generally stored their treasures in a coin cabinet, a substantial piece of furniture in its own right. Splendid examples with marquetry doors and elegant cabriole legs come up at auction from time to time, and cost the earth, but plainer examples turn up occasionally in second-hand furniture stores, and as there is little general demand for them you might be lucky and get a bargain.

There are still specialist cabinet makers who produce modern coin cabinets in air-dried mahogany, walnut or rosewood (never oak, cedar or any highly resinous timber, which would react chemically with the contents). These cabinets have tiers of shallow drawers containing felt-based trays made of the same wood but with half-drilled holes of various diameters, suitable for every size of coin from the smallest copper to

Above: A souvenir wallet produced by the Royal Mint in 1968 to publicize the introduction of decimal coinage in 1971.

the largest crowns and dollars. As these cabinets are largely constructed by hand, they are more expensive than machine-made furniture, but prices vary widely, depending on size, number of drawers and such refinements as lockable double doors and brass fittings. Certainly, budget options exist.

The smaller cabinets will sit comfortably on a stout table (bear in mind the weight of the contents), but the more expensive versions are free-standing. When the doors are shut, these cabinets look no different from a drinks or television cabinet and can stand discreetly in your living room without attracting undue attention.

Hidden Dangers of PVC

PVC, once the preferred medium for sleeves, is not chemically inert. After a year or two, coins inserted in these sleeves begin to change their colour and appearance. Bronze coins turn green while "silver" turns to "gold", or, rather, acquires a sickly yellow slime. Thankfully, the rigid pages of albums are now plasticizer-free.

USING GUIDES AND CATALOGUES

Books dealing with aspects of coins and money have been in existence for many centuries, but in the past hundred years the spate of literature devoted to the subject has been enormous. There are thousands of books now available, ranging from beginners' guides to the subject to detailed studies of a single coin or series.

The old maxim "Knowledge pays off" is seldom truer than in the case of coin collecting and trading. A study of the literature appropriate to your chosen field will repay you handsomely. Coin dealers are very knowledgeable people, but numismatics is such a vast subject that no one could ever know everything. The money laid out on buying up-to-date catalogues alone will soon show an excellent return on the investment.

CATALOGUES

The essential tools that no collector should be without are the coin catalogues. Not so many years ago numismatics lagged behind philately in the provision of good catalogues covering the whole world, but this

Below: Comprehensive catalogues even include entries on contemporary imitations of coins, such as this poor copy of a George II halfpenny dated 1758 (top) and unofficial patterns, such as this issue portraying Edward VIII (bottom), released specifically for collectors years after his abdication.

Right: Popular contemporary coin literature ranges from the massive, and indispensable, compendia on coins of the world, published by the American company Krause (top of picture), to smaller guides detailing the coins of single countries, and specialist periodials and catalogues.

deficiency has been remedied by the splendid range now published by Krause Publications of Iola, Wisconsin.

It may seem strange that a small town in the American Midwest should be the centre of a publishing concern of global stature, but the *vade mecum* for most collectors is Krause's *Standard Catalog of World Coins*, published annually. It started out in 1972 as a single volume encompassing all the coins of the modern world, from about 1800 onward. Today it has expanded back in time to 1600 as well as right up to the present day and has been divided into four volumes, covering the 17th, 18th, 19th and 20th centuries respectively. Each of the current volumes is thicker than a London or New York telephone directory. Along the way the "phone book" (as it is affectionately known the world over) has spawned a range of more detailed catalogues, dealing with specific countries or periods

The Krause catalogues are in a class of their own, but at the next level there is an enormous range of rivals that concentrate on single countries or periods. In the USA, for example, the collector has the choice of several excellent works such as *The Handbook of United States Coins* (known as the "Blue Book"), and

The Guide Book of United States Coins, (known as the "Red Book"), both issued by Whitman Publishing of Atlanta.

In Britain the pre-eminent catalogues are those formerly published by B.A. Seaby but now kept up to date under the imprint of Spink & Son. These catalogues group coins by reign, but a different approach has been adopted by the Coincraft *Standard Catalogues,* in which coins are classified according to denomination. These two radically different approaches reflect the contrasting ways in which coins are collected and studied.

Below: Specialist catalogues may not tell the full story about mintage and availability of coins.

There are authoritative specialized coin catalogues for virtually every country now, most of them compiled and published in the countries concerned. Although many are not in English, they are generally well illustrated and include a glossary of terms in different languages, so using them is not difficult. Besides, the collector who wishes to concentrate on the coins of France or Germany, for example, will very soon acquire a working knowledge of the relevant language anyway.

A number of catalogue producers also publish yearbooks, which generally incorporate price guides as well as containing a wealth of other reference material. Auction catalogues for sales of important collections are invariably well illustrated, with scholarly descriptions of each lot, and these are much prized as permanent reference works.

CATALOGUE PRICES

A salient feature of catalogues is that they contain prices, which gives the collector a pretty good guide to current market values. Some catalogues are published by dealers, and so the prices are essentially those at which coins in the different grades are offered for sale. Most catalogues, however, are produced by a team of dealers and experts and the prices quoted tend to reflect the prevailing state of the market more accurately and objectively.

Catalogues often include mintage figures, which can give a pointer to the relative scarcity of a coin, although these statistics have to be used with caution for they seldom take account of the vast quantities of coins melted down by the mints and therefore do not truly reflect the availability of material on the market.

WHERE TO FIND OUT MORE

Whereas catalogues tend to set out the bare details of coins with prices alongside, handbooks have a more discursive approach. Most of them do not provide prices (which would soon be rendered obsolete) but are designed as monographs that will stand the test of time. In this category come the sumptuous series published by the British Museum

Above: Try an on-line numismatic book store for helpful guides.

over more than a century, and now running to many volumes, dealing in considerable depth with the coins of Greece and Rome.

An impressive runner-up is the series compiled by members of the British and Royal Numismatic Societies and published under the generic title of *Sylloge of Coins of the British Isles,* which has been in progress since 1958. It started out as volumes that catalogued in detail the coins in the great national collections, beginning with the Fitzwilliam Museum in Cambridge and the Hunterian Museum in Glasgow. Ignoring the British Museum collections (which were already well-documented) apart from the Hiberno-Norse series, it covered the collections of other provincial museums in the British Isles, but also recorded British coins in the leading European and American museums and has latterly concentrated on the great private collections such as those formed by Emery Norweb, R.P. Mack and John Brooker. These handsome volumes were originally published by the British Academy but have recently been issued by Spink.

Browsing through these scholarly works makes you realize the complexities of British coins alone – and these are a drop in the ocean compared with the coinage output of the whole world. There is now a definitive handbook for just about anything, no matter how esoteric, from the *Pobjoy Encyclopedia of Isle of Man Coins and Tokens* (1977) to *Jewish Ghettos' and Concentration Camps' Money* by Zvi Stahl (1990).

International Coin Literature

The main English-language periodicals for coin collectors are published in the USA: *COINage* (Miller, Ventura, California), *Coin World* (Amos Press, Sidney, Ohio) and *World Coin News*, (Krause, Iola, Wisconsin). Krause also publish a range of more specialized titles such as *Coin Prices* and *Coins and Numismatic News*. America also takes the lead with *Celator* (Lancaster, Pennsylvania), the only magazine aimed specifically at collectors of ancient coins. *Canadian Coin News* (Trajan, St Catharine's, Ontario) and *Coin News* (Token Publishing, Honiton, England) also have a worldwide readership. *Cronica Numismatica* (Domfil, Barcelona), *El Eco* (Vilanova) and *Cronaca Numismatica* (Bolaffi, Rome) are the leading magazines in Spanish and Italian, while *Revue Numismatique* and *Numismatique et Change* (Paris), *Münzen und Medaillen* (Berlin), *Münzen Revue* (Switzerland) and *Money Trend* (Vienna) serve French and German collectors respectively. *Munt Kourier* is published for collectors in the Netherlands.

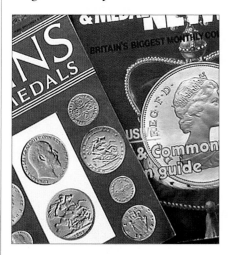

COLLECTING BY COUNTRY

Traditionally, collectors have naturally tended to concentrate on the coins of their own country as the most readily available. They would begin with the coins they encountered in their small change in everyday life, gradually exchanging worn specimens for examples in better condition. Then they would work backwards in time, seeking examples of obsolete coins in second-hand or junk shops. Finally, they would begin buying from coin dealers and auctions to fill the gaps in the older issues; coins of a previous regime or those pre-dating economic upheavals and monetary reforms.

This is probably still the usual approach to coin collecting, but the rise of mail-order and on-line trading has made the choice infinitely wider. It is

now feasible for even the novice collector to acquire coins from any country that appeals on account of the diversity of its coinage, the type of coins or the subjects pictured on them.

CHOOSING A COUNTRY

Many collectors are attracted to a particular area for religious reasons. Thus the coins of Israel have an immense appeal to Jewish collectors all over the world. Similarly, Catholics are drawn to the beautiful and prolific issues of the Vatican City State. In both cases, there is infinite scope in the earlier coinage, on the one hand that of Judaea and the Nabatean kingdom as well as the coins of the Jewish revolts against Roman rule, and on the other the fascinating coins of the Papacy stretching back to early medieval times.

As the collection becomes more advanced, the collector may wish to narrow the scope to a single period or reign and concentrate on different coin types, die variants and mint-marks. Hand in hand with the amassing of

Right: Ireland's history has been chronicled in coins: (clockwise from top left) the Hiberno-Norse penny, a Henry VIII "Harp" groot, a "Gun-money" half crown of James II, a halfpenny of William and Mary, a halfpenny struck during the Siege of Limerick, and the "St Patrick" farthing of Charles II.

Above: The more research you do into the coinage of your chosen country, the better idea you will have of what is available to collect.

specimens goes the study of the history, geography, economic structure and monetary policies of the area, all factors that have an impact on the size, choice of metal or denomination of the coins at different times, not to mention the portraits of rulers and changes to inscriptions and armorial devices.

Other factors that may have some bearing on the choice of country may include the frequency of issue and the

Below: If the coins of a country run into thousands, you can opt to focus on the output of a specific region, such as these coins of Bengal: post-Gupta coins (top) struck under the authority of Sasanka, King of Gauda, 600–630; silver tankas of the Sultans of Bengal (middle); and gold mohurs of the East India Company, Bengal Presidency, struck at the Calcutta Mint (bottom).

balance between the definitive series and the number of commemorative or special issues. In general, the latter are phenomena belonging to the past half century, but even the most conservative coin-issuing countries seem to be producing more and more of these coins, which are essentially intended for the collectors' market rather than for general circulation.

THE IRISH EXAMPLE

When considering the variety of definitive issues you will find countries such as San Marino, which changes its designs each year, at one extreme and at the other countries such as the USA, whose basic series has remained unchanged for many years. In the middle are countries whose modern coinage does not go back very far, has not changed much since its inception, and which does not include too many special issues. These can be useful building blocks for putting together a comprehensive but not complex single-country collection.

A good example of this is provided by Ireland, whose modern coinage began in 1928 with a harp obverse and various animals on the reverses. Apart from the change of Gaelic title in 1939,

Above and left: The inscribed names on the 20th-century coins of Congo, Central Africa, chronicle its transition from French colony to People's Republic.

when "Saorstat Eireann" (Irish Free State) was replaced by "Eire" (Ireland), the Barnyard series continued until the advent of decimal currency in 1971. On the decimal coins, the harp obverse remained the same, and the animal motifs were retained on the cupro-nickel coins; only the bronze low values were given new reverse designs, based on ancient Celtic art, in a series that continued until Ireland adopted the euro in 2002.

Only a handful of Irish special issues have appeared since 1966. On the other hand, Ireland has a numismatic history that stretches back more than a thousand years to the Norse kingdom of Dublin. Interesting coins for collectors include the Anglo-Irish pennies, the "gun money" of the Williamite Wars and the tokens and coppers of the 18th and early 19th centuries.

THE INDIAN EXAMPLE

Apart from the usual country approach, many collectors in earlier generations gravitated towards the coins of ancient Greece and Rome. In the 1950s an interest in the Byzantine series began to develop, and recently an increasing number of collectors worldwide have been focusing on Islamic coinage, which had, naturally, always been popular with Muslim collectors. Now the

numerous issues of the dynasties of the Indian subcontinent are attracting a growing following outside India. It is interesting that, while Greek and Roman coins appealed to early collectors everywhere because they had all received a classical education, the attraction of Islamic or Indian coins is also transcending the barriers of race, religion or language, the lure of the relatively unfamiliar being a large part of their appeal.

CHANGING BORDERS

Sometimes it is difficult to define the scope of a country from the collector's standpoint. In Europe there have been sweeping changes in the latter part of the last century, as a result of the reunification of Germany on the one hand and on the other the fragmentation of the USSR, Yugoslavia and even Czechoslovakia, resulting in many new names appearing in the coin catalogues.

The political changes in Africa have seen many former colonial territories adopting new names. The Congo is a particularly confusing example: the former Belgian Congo became the Democratic Republic of the Congo (1960), then Zaire (1977) and is now the Democratic Republic once more (since 1999). The neighbouring French Congo became the Popular Republic of the Congo and issued coins thus designated until 1993, when the name was changed to the Republic of the Congo.

It is important to note that most general catalogues list coins only from the 18th century onward. The collector delving into the coins of earlier periods therefore has to seek out more specialized handbooks and monographs to get the full story.

Above: Mints now produce country-themed sets of coins to tempt collectors and promote tourism.

Island Coinage

Another fairly manageable group that has considerable appeal is the Pacific islands. Apart from Hawaii (which had its own coins only in the 19th century) and former German New Guinea (pictured), none of these territories has a history of distinctive coinage going back before World War II, and in most cases their coins have only appeared within recent years.

COLLECTING BY GROUP

Rather than concentrating on the coins of a single country, many collectors prefer to study the coins of a group of territories that are related to each other, either geographically or politically. This might mean countries that have a shared colonial or Commonwealth history, or neighbouring countries with a shared language or culture. This approach provides more variety and interest in the collection generally, as well as allowing the collector to develop the theme of common interest, even exploring links in the design and production of the coins themselves.

SHARED IDENTITIES

A prime example of the geopolitical approach is to take a group of modern countries that, on account of their contiguity, have much in common, which is reflected in the development of their coinage. The Scandinavian countries – Denmark, Norway, Sweden and

Below: The "C5" monogram of Christian V of Denmark and Norway (1670–99) appears on the coins of both of these territories (top and middle). Christian V and his son Frederick IV appeared on the same coin of 1699 (bottom), Frederick on the obverse.

Above: Examples of religious imagery include a small cross on both sides of a coin of Canute (top), the hand of God on a penny of Aethelred (middle) and highly pictorial Christian imagery on a Habsburg thaler of Joseph II (bottom).

Finland – provide considerable scope for this kind of treatment. They have a shared cultural heritage, similar languages and a history that has frequently been intertwined.

Although they developed as separate kingdoms they were actually united under Margrethe I of Denmark (1387–1412) in a federation known as the Union of Kalmar. This lasted until 1523 when Gustav Vasa expelled the Danes from Sweden and founded a separate dynasty. Finland remained under Swedish rule until 1809, when it was ceded to Russia and became a separate grand duchy under the tsar.

When Finland gained its independence in 1917 it was the lion rampant emblem of the Vasa kings that became the motif on the coinage. Linguistically, Finland belongs to the Finno-Ugric group (which includes Estonia and Hungary) but there is still a large minority of inhabitants who are linguistically and ethnically Swedish, and ties across the Baltic remain strong.

American Colonial Coins

John Hull and Robert Saunderson operated a mint in Boston, which struck the first American coinage long before the United States gained independence from Britain. It was simply inscribed "NE" (New England) with denominations in Roman numerals, and was followed by coins featuring willow, pine (pictured) or oak trees. The Willow Tree shilling first appeared in 1652, but the other tree designs were not issued until the following decade. However, they all bore that original date to get around the fact that they had not been authorized by Charles II. Maryland, New York, New Jersey and Connecticut also produced coins during this period.

Norway was ceded by Denmark to Sweden in 1814, but resistance from Norwegian nationalists led to its rule as a separate kingdom under the Swedish crown until 1905, when it became a wholly independent sovereign state under Haakon VII, a Danish prince. Ties between the Scandinavian countries were strengthened by the adoption of a common currency based on the krona of 100 öre in 1875.

Below: Russian coinage of 1757 bore the arms of its conquered Baltic kingdoms, Livonia and Estonia.

THE LOW COUNTRIES

Belgium, the Netherlands and Luxembourg are another obvious choice for the subject of a group collection. Today they are separate countries, but they have a common history going back thousands of years to the time when they were settled by the Belgae, a Celtic people.

In the Middle Ages they formed the core of the duchy of Burgundy, which fell under Habsburg rule in the 1490s. The northern part broke away in the 1570s to form the United Provinces (now Holland) while the south became the Austrian Netherlands. By the Congress of Vienna (1815) the whole of the Netherlands was united under the king of Holland, but Belgium seceded in 1830 and Luxembourg was separated from Holland in 1890. Ties remained close and in 1945 they formed a commercial union (Benelux), a forerunner of, and model for, the European Union. Belgium and Luxembourg have had similar currencies (both struck at Brussels) and all three have issued coins in similar designs to commemorate events of common interest.

IMPERIAL COINS

The former territories of the French, Portuguese and British colonial empires are areas with strong political links. The French and Portuguese tended to use uniform motifs for their dependent territories, whereas apart from the profile of the reigning monarch, coins of the dominions and colonies of the British Empire, and later of the Commonwealth, were quite distinctive in their reverse types.

Then there are the colonies that federated. They would have enjoyed their own coins prior to uniting, and thus the colonial coinage can be collected as a separate entity, with or without the coins of the united country. There are quite a number of instances of this, the coins in each case varying considerably in scarcity and expense. At one end of the scale there are the coins of the

Above (clockwise from top left): United Provinces klippe, cut peso from Curaçao, gulden of the Dutch West Indies and thaler of the Austrian Netherlands.

American colonies produced in Massachusetts (1652), Maryland (1659) and New Jersey (1682), followed by the "Rosa Americana" series struck by William Wood at Bath in the early 18th century. Even after the Declaration of Independence in 1776, distinctive coins were circulating in Connecticut, Massachusetts, New Hampshire, New Jersey, New York and Vermont. Some of them were very similar to their British counterparts, with Britannia on the reverse but replacing the effigy of George III with George Washington or a Native American. From 1776 onward there were also various attempts at federal issues, such as the "Nova Constellatio" coppers and the "Fugio" cents, before the emergence of the Federal coinage in 1792. If the numerous tokens that also circulated in the late 18th century were also included, this would be a formidable group indeed.

A similar pattern obtained in British North America, where local issues, mainly bank tokens, were produced in Upper and Lower Canada (modern Ontario and Quebec), New Brunswick, Nova Scotia and Prince Edward Island, before the Confederation in 1867. Prince Edward Island continued to issue its own coins until it joined the Confederation in 1873; Newfoundland had its own coins, until 1947.

Above: A Dutch coin weight being used in the Caribbean. The Dutch economy was boosted by its involvement in the sugar and tobacco plantations there.

RELIGIOUS SYMBOLISM

Just as coins of the Islamic world conformed in design to the belief systems of that religion, across Christendom coins used a common Christian imagery, sometimes in a bid to convert pagans to Christianity and, later, Catholics to Protestantism.

Christian iconography was prevalent on Byzantine coinage, while in northwestern Europe subtle religious symbols appeared on coins in the territories subject to Anglo-Saxon influence. In Scandinavia, prior to the Viking Age, Harald Bluetooth employed Christian symbols on coins as a part of his efforts to convert the Danes. A handful of very rare coins produced around the first millennium depict brooding symbols of divine judgment, such as the hand of God on the English coins of Aelthelred. Nordic and Anglo-Saxon coins were again united in Christian symbolism by the imperial coins of King Canute, which featured the crucifix. This ubiquitous religious icon dominated the "Long-cross" and "Short-cross" pennies that circulated in Britain for centuries.

In later medieval times, Christian imagery was employed to highly picturesque effect on the coins of the great city states of the Habsburg Empire, and also on Italian coins such as those of Venice and the Papacy in Rome.

COLLECTING BY MINT

As an alternative to collecting coins of a particular country, a number of collectors are now examining some interesting and challenging alternatives. Such lateral thinking allows you to cut across national frontiers and find common factors to shape a collection. An obvious one is to study and collect the products of a particular mint. In most cases the larger mints (such as those operated under the US Treasury Department) produce coins only for their own country, or operate on such a global scale that the field would be far too wide, but others make interesting subjects for collections. Some mints have gained contracts to produce coins for territories too small to have their own national mint.

COLLECTING BY MINT-MARK

Collecting coins according to mint can stretch back to the time of the Roman Empire. Many collectors of classical coins, for example, concentrate on the imperial coins struck at the Roman mints in Alexandria, Carthage, Serdica, Constantinople or western Europe. All are clearly identifiable by their mint-marks and inscriptions.

At the other end of the spectrum you could concentrate on the coins that emanated from a particular mint in a

Below: Imperial Roman coins bearing the mint-marks of Nikomedia (SMN), in what is now Turkey, and Treverorum (TROBS), now Trier in Germany.

Above: Coins minted by royalist factions during the English Civil War had their own inscriptions, ranging from monograms such as "BR" on coins of the Bristol Mint (top), to motifs such as Oxford plumes on coins of that city (middle) and a lion of York (bottom).

country where several mints were in simultaneous operation. This might, for example, mean confining your interest to coins bearing the S mark of San Francisco, the aqueduct mark of Segovia in Spain, or the letters A or D that identify coins from Berlin or Munich respectively.

During the English Civil War the Parliamentary forces controlled the mint at the Tower of London. This meant that the Royalists were obliged to rely on various temporary mints established at Aberystwyth, Shrewsbury or Oxford and later mints in a few pockets of resistance and Royalist strongholds such as Chester, Exeter, Truro and York. Identifiable coins from these places are much sought after by those occupied in collecting the antiquities of their own town or county, quite apart from their general numismatic interest.

Above: The Birmingham Mint was established in 1860 by Matthew Boulton. It still produces coinage, tokens and medals – like this commemorative issue for the mint itself – for the international numismatic market.

PRIVATE MINTS

This leaves the private mints, which, not being tied to national contracts, offer their services to any country or issuing authority that cares to use them. At one time the Birmingham Mint, the successor to Boulton & Watt's Soho Mint, later known as the Heaton Mint, struck coins for well over a hundred governments from Afghanistan (1886) to Zambia (1968). The company produced the first issues of many countries, from Chile in 1851 and

---

Perth Mint

The Perth Mint remained under the jurisdiction of the Royal Mint until 1970, where it was transferred to the authority of the Government of Western Australia. Today the mint still operates from its original building, constructed from limestone extracted from the offshore Western Australian island of Rottnest, and it is one of the oldest mints in the world to do so.

Above: Regional mint-marks on Spanish coins include the letters S for Seville (top), M for Madrid (middle) and B for Barcelona (bottom).

Above: The stunning limestone colonnaded building that houses the Perth Mint has stood on Hay Street in the east of the city since 1899.

Bulgaria in 1881 to the emergent states of the former British Empire in the 1950s and 1960s. Many of these coins bore the mint-mark H, including some British pennies subcontracted by the Royal Mint, but most were unmarked. Fortunately, the comprehensive records of this mint have documented every coin struck there. In the 1980s, it was still producing coins under subcontract from the Royal Mint, but nowadays its numismatic output is confined to

Below: The Royal Canadian Mint produces coins for the native country and other territories around the world. Like the Perth Mint, it is also involved in refining gold for coinage.

tokens and medals: the company has diversified into die-stamping and forging radiator grills for cars and casings for microwave ovens, among many other products.

The Franklin Mint of Philadelphia was founded by Joseph Segel in 1965 and a decade later was boasting that it was the largest private mint in the world. It made its business originally when the silver dollar vanished from the scene and the gambling casinos of Nevada urgently needed a substitute. Dollar-sized pieces were struck in an alloy called franklinium, which resembled silver, and in 1969 the firm got its first coinage contract. Eventually it struck coins for the Bahamas, Barbados, Belize, the British Virgin Islands, Jamaica, Panama, Trinidad and Tobago and Tunisia, but by 1975 it had largely switched to other areas including a wide range of collectables, from limited edition books to costume dolls.

PROLIFIC MINTS

The role of leading private mint then passed to a company founded by Ernest Pobjoy after World War II but which could trace its origins in die-sinking and medal-striking back to Birmingham in the late 17th century. In its early years this family firm made its reputation in the manufacture of badges, regalia and Masonic jewels, but with the development of automats and slot machines it developed a business

in tokens of all kinds. These may not be coins of the realm but they must be struck to a very precise specification for use in slot machines, and it was the development of this technology that placed Pobjoy at the forefront of the burgeoning medal market in the 1960s, notably producing the sets commemorating Sir Winston Churchill (1965) and the Apollo moon landing (1969).

Another key player in the market for bullion coins and collectable editions is the Perth Mint in Western Australia. Originally a branch of the Royal Mint, it went into operation in 1899, two years before Australia's five states, which had previously functioned as separate colonies of the British Empire, were federated. The Perth Mint was established by the Australian government in response to the need to convert nationally mined gold into real currency that could be exchanged within the Western territory. During its 100 years of operation, the mint has been instrumental both in the refinement of gold into ingots and in minting circulating coins. Its refining wing was merged with a select group of private companies in the late 1990s, and this now operates separately from the state-run mint, which continues to pioneer interesting coins.

COLLECTING BY PERIOD

Focusing on the coins of a particular era presents the collector with a great opportunity to explore historical interests. There are many different options for collecting by period. You can collect the coins of a particular reign or political regime, or you can study coins belonging to several countries involved in a religious, political or monetary upheaval, such as the countries affected by colonial ambition or religious crusades; the 20th-century victims of Nazi aggression; the effects of high inflation on the coins of Central Europe after World War I, or the economic struggles of Latin American countries in more recent years.

PERIOD OF OFFICE
You might pick on the coins that were issued during the term of office of a particular head of state. The coins struck by the US Mint and its branches lend themselves well to this approach.

You could consider the variations in coinage that appeared during the periods of office of certain presidents, such as James Madison (1809–17) or

Below: Imperial coins of George V produced for Southern Rhodesia (top), Canada (middle) and Cyprus (bottom).

Above: US presidents (clockwise from top left) Grant, Lincoln, Eisenhower, Roosevelt and Washington.

Andrew Jackson (1829–37). Even the brief presidency of Zachary Taylor (1849–50) is worth considering, as a lot of changes took place in that period. The two terms of Ulysses S. Grant (1869–77) were also extremely eventful, not least because the American economy was beginning to recover and expand in the aftermath of the Civil War, and this is reflected in coinage.

Undoubtedly, the most prolific coinage, in terms of different denominations, new types, dates and mintmarks, was the record presidency of Franklin D. Roosevelt (1932–45), whose four terms spanned the Depression years and World War II. A mark of the respect in which he was held was the prompt change of the dime soon after his death. The choice of this coin was singularly appropriate as Roosevelt, himself a victim of polio, inaugurated the March of Dimes, a nationwide fundraising campaign to combat polio and care for its victims.

REGAL COINS
The monarchical approach can offer even greater scope, for kings and queens have often reigned for very long periods and in some cases coins bearing their effigies were issued in overseas colonies and dominions, as well as in their own country.

It would probably be well-nigh impossible to collect all the coins that bear one or other of the effigies of Elizabeth II, which, introduced in 1953, have now been around for more than half a century. During this long period many colonies and protectorates that had quite happily got by with coins of the mother country attained independence and introduced coins of their own. While many of these territories are now republics whose coins portray their own presidents, as head of the Commonwealth the Queen's portrait may still be found not only on the current coins of the "old dominions" such as Australia, Canada and New Zealand, but also on those of many other, newer countries, from Antigua and Ascension to Tuvalu and Zambia.

ECONOMIC UPHEAVAL

The coinage of the world in modern times (which, in the numismatic sense, began with the 16th century) was relatively stable until World War I. When war broke out in August 1914, Britain hastily withdrew gold coins from circulation and introduced Treasury notes as a temporary measure. Like income tax (a temporary measure at the time of the Napoleonic Wars), this expedient became permanent and gold has never circulated in Britain since.

This did not end the production of gold sovereigns, for they were still required overseas, but at certain periods in Britain it was illegal to possess more than two examples of the same gold coin (this concession enabled bona fide collectors to keep examples showing both obverse and reverse side by side), and during the early 1970s it was illegal for unauthorized persons to hold gold coins of any kind. Other countries have placed similar restrictions on gold at various times. Ironically, there are probably more gold coins being minted than ever before, as well as a plethora of gold bullion pieces, though none sees general circulation owing to the high (and fluctuating) value of gold.

Below: Crusader coins include a 12th-century George and Dragon copper follis of Antioch (top), a 13th-century Aleppo dirham with a star motif imitating Ayyubid design (middle) and a silver gros of Bohemond VI, struck in Tripoli.

Above: American troops arrive in Germany at the close of World War I.

Below: The 10 pfennig coin of Duren, one of many German towns that issued local coins during and just after World War I. Due to inflation, these coins had a very short life and were replaced by Notgeld (emergency paper money).

While a collection of gold coins can illustrate the vagaries of monetary practice, a popular aspect of numismatics is concerned with the rise of inflation and its impact on coinage. Again, this was largely a product of World War I, although it began with people hoarding silver and gold coins. Even base metal coins disappeared from circulation, giving rise to the local tokens described as "money of necessity". The war's immediate effect on coins, however, was the replacement of bronze and brass (required for the manufacture of shell cases) by zinc, iron or steel. This expedient was resuscitated in World War II, particularly in countries under Nazi occupation (which themselves would be an interesting subject for a coin collection).

Inflation at other times has led to frequent changes in the coinage of such countries as Iceland and Israel. It was a chronic problem in Latin American countries, and although it can be spectacularly illustrated with the colourful and prolific banknotes of the period it can also be traced in the debasement and diminution of the coins.

CRUSADER COINS

The coinage of occupied Europe in both World Wars is a good subject, with a wealth of readily accessible material for study, but many centuries earlier there was another period that resulted in some fascinating coins. In spring 1095 the Byzantine emperor Alexius I Comnenus appealed to Pope Urban II to raise an army to liberate the Holy Land from the clutches of Islam. Thus began the extraordinary but poorly understood period in history known as the Crusades.

The Crusader coins mirrored their European contemporaries but were strongly influenced by Byzantine and Islamic models. Thus, the Kingdom of Jerusalem produced a lengthy series of gold bezants, silver deniers and billon obols, while the Principality of Antioch struck copper folles and billon deniers from 1100 to 1268. The County of Tripoli (1095–1289) had gold bezants, silver gros, billon deniers and copper obols, as well as drachmae and half drachmae in the 13th century. Copper coins of various sizes were issued at Edessa between 1098 and the mid-12th century, mainly in the names of successive kings of Jerusalem, although Tancred of Sicily, Prince of Antioch, struck coins in 1104.

Asssociated with the coins of these Crusader states were the Frankish coins in Cyprus, which, nominally part of the Byzantine Empire, was a separate fiefdom carved out by Guy de Lusignan in 1192, after he was deposed from the throne of Jerusalem. His successor, Aimery de Lusignan, declared himself king in 1197, and from then until 1324 monarchs were styled as Kings of Cyprus and Jerusalem. In addition to coins in copper (of which there was a natural abundance), the rulers of Cyprus struck "white bezants" in 8 carat gold. Also in this category are the coins of the Latin Empire of Constantinople itself (1204–61).

COLLECTING BY DENOMINATION

A possible departure from the tradition of collecting coins by country or period is to group them according to their denomination or face value. When focusing on coins of a particular size or type within a country, this approach is basically an extension of one-country specialization, but it becomes infinitely more varied and interesting to trace the development and spread of one kind of coin across a continent or, indeed, the entire world.

You can concentrate on "minors" such as cents and farthings, or major coins such as dollars and crowns. Some denominations have had a particularly long history, providing scope for discussion of changes to profile and value.

BUILDING A DOLLAR-THEMED COLLECTION

The dollar – still the world's most popular denomination and the currency of choice in many countries – is a very well-travelled example. Its early history,

Below: A collection of US dollars might be organized around those featuring Native Americans (Missouri centennial half dollar of 1921, top, and 1908 Indian head gold eagle, middle left), or portraits of Liberty in profile (1795 dollar, middle right), seated (1862 half dollar, bottom left) or standing (1908 gold 20 dollars, bottom right).

in fierce competition with other trade currencies, was beset with difficulties and false starts.

COLLECTING SILVER DOLLARS

Over the years there were many types of silver dollar, from the original Liberty heads with flowing hair or draped bust and heraldic eagle to the seated Liberty types whose eagle reverse is found with or without a motto. Production of ordinary dollars ceased in 1873, but trade dollars with a seated Liberty facing left and an eagle that also looked the other way filled the gap. Ordinary dollars were resumed in 1878 and continued until 1935. Production was then suspended as the silver dollar's place had been taken by the silver certificate. Coins of this type dated 1964 were struck at Denver but were never issued, and every example is believed to have been destroyed.

When dollar coins of the same diameter were revived in 1971, they were struck in .400 silver in uncirculated and proof versions, but those intended for general circulation had a copper core and a cupro-nickel cladding. Too large for everyday use, the dollar was reduced in size and re-emerged in 1979 as a 12-sided coin. In 2000 this was replaced by a larger, circular coin in a gold-coloured alloy portraying Sacagawea, the Indian guide to the Lewis and Clark Expedition.

MAKING ITS MARK

Prior to the foundation of the German Empire, in 1871, the mark existed only as money of account. It derived from the fine mark of Cologne, an expression of bullion that was widely accepted in the vast conglomeration of German states. It took several years to replace the thaler of 32 groschen used in the northern states, and the gulden of 90 kreuzer prevalent in the southern states, with a single monetary system based on the Reichsmark of 100 pfennige. A measure of compromise was

Above: The history of the German mark can be explored in the state coinage of Saxony from 1903 (top), coins of the Third Reich (middle) and the currency of East Germany, 1971 (bottom).

Left: The German mark began as a unit used only in money of account. This 19th-century German coin weight would have been used to determine weight.

reflected in the minting of 2 and 3 mark coins, equivalent to the obsolete gulden and thaler respectively, which continued until 1939.

The mark was a silver coin from its inception, in 1873, until 1916. It vanished from circulation during World War I and was engulfed by inflation in the immediate post-war period. In 1924–5 it re-emerged inscribed "1 Mark", swiftly followed by silver coins of 1925–7 inscribed "1 Reichsmark". From 1933 to 1939 the coin was struck in nickel. When it re-emerged in 1950 it was inscribed "1 Deutschemark".

Cupro-nickel coins with the inscription "Bundersrepublik Deutschland" (Federal Republic of Germany) on the obverse and the reverse showing the

Frequently Changing Designs

While most British coins in everyday use have had unchanged reverse motifs since decimalization in 1971, an exception is the pound coin, which has had a different reverse each year since its inception in 1983. The royal arms (1983) were followed by floral emblems of the four countries comprising the United Kingdom (1984–7), then heraldic motifs and, most recently, landmark bridges of Scotland (Forth railway bridge), Northern Ireland (Belfast–Dublin Railway), Wales (Menai Bridge) and England (Gateshead Millennium Bridge). Of these four architectural giants, the first three were built at various points during the 19th century, whereas the latter, which crosses the River Tyne in Newcastle, opened in 2000 and quickly became the pride of this northerly city.

Above: A "basic currency unit" collection centred on the British farthing might include a tin farthing issue of William and Mary (top) and the many imitative tokens (bottom).

Left: Pattern obverses of the recent series of pound coins, paired with their pictorial reverses. From left: the famous transport bridges of Scotland, Northern Ireland, Wales and England.

Above: The Greek drachma was an ancient currency unit, revived soon after Greece won its independence from Turkey.

value flanked by oak leaves, continued until the advent of the euro in 2001. With annual issues from up to six different mints, identifiable by a code letter, the major types of the mark would form a very large collection.

By contrast, coins with a very similar reverse, but struck in aluminium with the emblem of the German Democratic Republic on the obverse, were not adopted until 1956 and were very sporadically struck thereafter, reflecting the political division and economic disparity of the German states. The "Ostmark" disappeared when Germany was reunited in 1990. Both republics were prolific producers of 2, 5 and 10 mark coins for commemorative and special issues.

BASIC CURRENCY UNITS

Not everyone can afford to collect large, handsome silver dollars and crowns, and many numismatists focus on other, smaller denominations.

In England the "splendid shilling" of 12 pence sterling began with the testoon of Henry VII and survives today as the 5 pence in the decimal series, but it has undergone many changes of design, weight and composition over the centuries, as have its counterparts in the Commonwealth. Even the cent, usually the smallest coin in a currency range, offers immense scope, from humble US pennies to the

Below: Interesting and collectable ephemera often accompanies the introduction of a new denomination coin.

small bronze, steel or aluminium coins of many countries. Other minor issues include the öre coins of Scandinavia or the 1 and 5 centime coins of France. The humble pfennig of Germany was successively struck in copper, aluminium, bronze, zinc, bronze-clad steel and latterly copper-plated steel, reflecting the political and economic upheavals of the 20th century.

Such coins may have little or no spending power alone, but they are vital in making up odd amounts in everyday transactions. British numismatists have a special affection for the farthing (originally the fourth part of a penny). Redundant by 1956, many have survived in generally fine condition because people who got them in change tended to hoard them in jars. Similar hoarding of bronze cents in the USA caused a currency crisis in 1982 when the price of copper rose sharply, and the US Treasury was compelled to replace bronze by a zinc alloy.

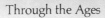

Through the Ages

The first £1 coin was minted in 1489 by Henry VIIth. It remained until the £1 note was established in 1915, although the first note had appeared briefly during the Napoleonic wars.

Maxwell House are very pleased to be able to present to you, as one of our special customers, a new £1 coin.

One of the most striking features of the new coin is the inscription on its milled edge "Decus et tutamen", quite unique on British coins. Roughly translated, this means "An ornament and a safeguard".

We hope you will treasure this £1 coin as a memento of this historic occasion.

Your New One Pound Coin

COLLECTING PICTORIAL COINS

While coin obverses have, traditionally, been reserved for portraits – either allegorical or symbolic figures or lifelike effigies of rulers – pictorial reverses have predominated on coins since the very earliest currencies. The splendid silver coins of 16th century Europe – guldengroschen and thaler – stimulated the development of sophisticated pictorial designs by virtue of their large size, and numismatic pictorialism may be said to have attained perfection during the 20th century.

Landmarks of national or religious significance featured on ancient coins and on some of the beautiful city coinage of medieval trading centres, and continue to be commemorated on some of the world's most recent issues. Mythical creatures such as winged deities or dragons have also featured heavily, due to their links with national folklore and identity. Animals – once symbolic of trade and economic strength – remain a popular pictorial theme, though in a world economy that relies more on mechanization than livestock they are now likely to represent a topic such as conservation. Since the 1930s, the fashion for pictorials has become increasingly linked with commemoratives and coins produced for the collectors' market.

Below: A cock and a crab on an ancient Sicilian coin (top), and images of a heraldic bear and lion on medieval coins of Germany and Zealand (bottom).

Above: Many Roman coins feature allegorical figures or landmarks (clockwise from top left): an allegorical depiction of the Tigris and Euphrates with Armenia; the Ara Pacis; a personification of "City" carrying two temples; the market on Caelian Hill.

TWO POSSIBLE APPROACHES

Two recent books, R.G. Penn's *Aspects of Medicine on Ancient Greek and Roman Coins* (Spink & Son, London, 1994) and Marvin Tameanko's *Monumental Coins: Buildings & Structures on Ancient Coinage* (Krause, Iola, 1999), explore two distinct branches of thematic coin-collecting. Tameanko, an architect, has concentrated on coins, mostly from Imperial Rome, that show identifiable buildings, such as temples, shrines, forts and triumphal arches, or engineering structures such as roadways, aqueducts and harbours. His book classifies more than 600 classical coins, featuring such landmarks as the Temple in Jerusalem, the Colosseum and the Acropolis. Two of the Seven Wonders of the World appear: the Pharos of Alexandria (the world's first lighthouse) and the Mausoleum of Halicarnassus, but it is strange that the Hellenistic kingdom of Egypt never depicted the Pyramids or the Sphinx on its coins.

Penn, a doctor of medicine, has adopted a rather different approach and used pictorial coins to illustrate the origins and development of medicine in the ancient world. Certain Greek coins portray Hippocrates and Asklepios (Aesculapius), the real and mythological fathers of medicine, and coins with mythological subjects that have a bearing on the ancient perception of illness and cures. Many coins of both Greek and Roman periods depict medicinal plants. There are also coins advocating sanitation, depicting the goddess Hygeia, healing springs and aqueducts, as well as the Cloaca Maxima (the great Roman sewer) and even Cloacina, goddess of the sewers.

Both these writers have brought to bear their professional expertise to write about their chosen coins. In the same way, many collectors develop a thematic collection that reflects their professional or recreational interests, giving numismatics a new dimension.

OTHER CLASSICAL SUBJECTS

Because so many Greek coins do not bear an inscription identifying their origin, there are books that catalogue them according to their subject-matter, and this has stimulated interest in collecting them in this manner. *Greek Coin Types and Their Identification* by Richard J. Plant (Spink & Son, 1979) is a notable example of this genre. While it was primarily intended as an

Below: Animals are closely linked with perceptions of national identity, and continue to be a popular pictorial subject on modern coins.

aid to identification, it serves as a very useful basis for a thematic collection. In it you can see at a glance the 116 coins showing Nike, the winged goddess of victory, or the numerous pieces that show helmeted warriors. The pantheon of Greek deities and associated heroes is set out clearly, from Aphrodite and Artemis to Zeus himself.

If animals are your choice, you can find coins showing animals fighting or feeding their young. In antiquity, bulls, either whole or in part, were a popular subject, perhaps an allusion to the value of cattle in the earliest barter economy, but dogs, wolves, sheep and goats are not far behind. Horses were a major subject, as were men on horseback or driving chariots and, of course, Pegasus the winged horse of mythology.

Lions, elephants, tigers and panthers form a veritable numismatic menagerie, while mythical beasts, such as the sphinx and the griffin, are also prominent. Eagles perching or in flight are a colossal subject, rivalling images of lions on coinage right down to the present day. Serpents, dolphins and fishes abound, as well as familiar flora.

Coins That Tell a Story
Several brass denarii of Vespasian and his son Titus have a reverse showing a date palm beneath which a woman sits weeping. To the left of the tree stands the emperor in armour, or a man with his hands tied behind his back – a captive taken in AD 70 when Titus suppressed a Jewish revolt, sacking Jerusalem and destroying the Temple. The sorrowful woman is an allegory for *Judaea capta* (captured) or *devicta* (defeated).

Above (clockwise from top-left): Coins have personified Africa, Helvetica, and Britannia both standing (middle) and seated (bottom), in female form.

MODERN PICTORIAL THEMES

The trend towards more pictorial reverses, which gathered momentum in the 1930s, yielded a good number of coins showing all kinds of shipping, from outrigger canoes to ocean-going liners. Although Germany struck some coins showing the Zeppelin airships, aviation as a theme only took off in 1983 with the celebration of the bicentenary of the first manned balloon flights; it received a tremendous boost in 2000–2, when many coins used the centenary of powered aircraft as an opportunity to show their development from the original Wright Flyer to Concorde. Both warships and military aircraft have been prominent in very recent years, on coins commemorating the military contingents fighting in World Wars and other conflicts.

Many contemporary coins are devoted to animals. Whereas earlier coins in this category merely showed them as typical examples of the fauna of a particular country, today the trend is didactic, highlighting species under threat of extinction. The People's Republic of China even launched its gold bullion series with motifs showing the giant panda, the elusive creature that has become the symbol of the World Wide Fund for Nature.

Above: A stunning medieval bishopric thaler of Münster (top), a landmark on a Turkish million lira coin and a temple on a Thai coin of Rama V.

Many pictorial coins are now issued in long thematic sets, which makes this kind of collecting all too easy. There is much more fun to be had in poring over coin catalogues, seeking out stray items on your favourite theme that will fit into your collection.

Above: This Iranian 1 rial coin is part of a series depicting mosques.

Below: A set of FAO coins issued by North Korea in 2002, depicting various modes of transport by land, sea and air.

COLLECTING PURPOSE OF ISSUE COINS

A major branch of thematic collecting is devoted to coins issued by several countries more or less simultaneously to celebrate a major anniversary of an event or personality of worldwide interest, or to publicize a contemporary event of global importance. These events are often the subject of colourful coins aimed at the collectors' market. The phenomenon of simultaneous or joint issues is relatively new, although there are some topics that, by their cyclical nature, have been the subject of coins from many countries at different times.

COMMEMORATIVES FOR COMMON PURPOSES

Philatelists describe issues by several countries celebrating the same event as omnibus issues. In numismatic terms the earliest instance of this occurred in 1617. The Thirty Years War, which split Europe on religious lines, was about to erupt when several states in Germany, Austria and Switzerland issued silver coins to celebrate the centenary of Martin Luther's Wittenberg Declaration, which launched the Reformation. Similar issues took place in 1717 and 1817. Even at the height of World War I, Saxony managed to

issue a silver 3 mark coin in 1917 under the auspices of the German Empire, but only 100 coins were struck, making this quatercentennial coin the key issue in any collection devoted to the Reformation. Sri Lanka marked 2500 years of Buddhism in 1957 with a set of coins.

BIRTHS, MARRIAGES AND DEATHS

Diana, Princess of Wales, was not the first international figure to be remembered by coins of more than one country. That honour went to John F. Kennedy, who not only replaced Benjamin Franklin on the American half dollar but was also portrayed on a silver 5 riyal coin issued by Sharjah, a remarkable feat since this Gulf sheikhdom had never issued any coins previously and by this gesture flew in the face of the Islamic ban on human representation in any form. The precedent was soon followed by other Gulf States, which produced coins portraying the late President Nasser of Egypt. The portrayal of famous persons, either soon after their death (as in the case of Pope John Paul II) or on a major anniversary, such as a centenary, has now become commonplace.

Above: Austria marked the bicentenary of Mozart's birth with this 1956 coin.

SPORTING EVENTS

Arguably the most important of all events in the numismatic calendar are those pertaining to sports. If shooting is counted as a sport, some of the earliest coins on this theme are those produced in the German states and Switzerland from 1590 onward, as prizes for annual shooting contests. They endured longest in Switzerland, where silver 5 francs and gold 100 francs were struck on behalf of various cantons as late as 1939, Lucerne being the last canton to issue them.

However, the Olympic Games tower over all other sporting events. As long ago as 510 BC distinctive coins for the Games were struck by Elis, the host state. By 480 BC coins showing the winged figure of Nike (Victory) alluded to the athletes who won the events. It is believed that the beautiful large decadrachms of Syracuse dating from about 465 BC were intended as prizes for athletes at the Demareteian Games.

The modern Olympic Games were inaugurated at Athens in 1896, but it was not until they were held in Helsinki that Finland produced special coins in 1951–2 showing the Olympic rings. Since then it has become axiomatic that coins marking the Games are released by the host country, often in lengthy series. Since the 1970s, special coins have also been released by many of the participating countries as well, with separate issues for the Winter Games and Paralympics.

Right: Popular sporting events celebrated on coins include the European and World Cup football championships.

Below: Classical subjects on coins marking the Olympic Games of Berlin (1936) and Athens (2004).

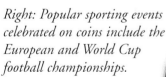
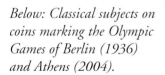

Left: Silver coins from the Isle of Man celebrate British royal family events; a multicoloured memorial issue for Pope John Paul II was produced in 2005.

MILITARY ANNIVERSARIES

The end of World War II, in 1945, did not trigger off any celebratory coins for victory or peace, but in recent years the 50th and 60th anniversaries of D-Day and VE Day have precipitated widespread issues, mainly of dollar-sized coins, while coins have also marked the anniversaries of liberation, the Battle of Britain and other campaigns or individual battles. This has become a formidable subject that seems likely to prompt new issues every few years.

The nostalgia has now begun to extend to the events and anniversaries of World War I and other conflicts. Both Australia and New Zealand have issued coins to mark anniversaries of the ANZAC involvement in the ill-fated Gallipoli campaign of 1915. Czechoslovakia (and now both the Czech Republic and Slovakia), as well as Poland and the former Soviet Union, have produced a number of coins marking battles and campaigns of World War II.

ANNUAL COINS

Special coins celebrating Christmas began to appear in the 1970s but have been confined to the Isle of Man and Tonga, issuing genre and religious subjects respectively. An exception to this, however, occurred in 2000 when many countries marked the end of the second millennium with special coins.

Of much wider popularity are the coins that celebrate the lunar New Year and have reverse motifs depicting the animals of the Chinese zodiac. These coins originated in China, Hong Kong and Macao, but the practice has since spread to other parts of the world. Struck in silver or gold as well as base metal, they are often exchanged as New Year gifts.

Lunar New Year

An Australian silver bullion coin featuring a golden retriever was struck by the Perth Mint to celebrate the Year of the Dog (February 2006). The ideogram for the year appears at the top with the date at the side and the weight and fineness of the silver at the foot. The presentation set included a silver-plated pin of a matching design.

Below: This pattern 140 ecu coin from the Isle of Man, showing a Viking ship, was produced when the ecu seemed to be the likely European coin, though later the euro was adopted instead.

Below: A crown from the Isle of Man ingeniously celebrating the Millennium with the centuries from 1000 to 2000 around the edge and a clock ticking away the seconds to the Millennium.

Below: Many German states, such as Mecklenburg-Schwerim (top), produced coins for royal weddings. A porcelain issue (bottom) produced in Germany to mark the Occupation of Singapore.

COLLECTING SERVICE TOKENS

We have already seen how "token" coinage was issued as a replacement for legitimate currency during periods where the latter was in short supply. However, tokens also exist that do not have a cash value, but nevertheless have a real worth in so far as they represent a specific service and are used in exchange for that service. In some cases they also represent value by being expressed in certain small commodities. This aspect of tokens was once neglected but they are now avidly collected and studied, often as an adjunct to the study of local history.

Below: An Australian brass token for use in amusement centres and a Canadian token giving a humorous spin on the practice of tossing a coin.

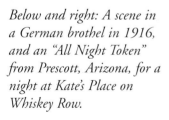

Below and right: A scene in a German brothel in 1916, and an "All Night Token" from Prescott, Arizona, for a night at Kate's Place on Whiskey Row.

Above: Numbered Industrial Surveys security token with police telephone number and instructions to the finder to return it to the nearest police station.

Below: Replicas of pre-decimal British coins used in the souvenir shop at Ironbridge Gorge, England.

One of the main reasons for these tokens is security; as they have no cash value, they cannot be spent and therefore do not present any temptation to would-be thieves.

BROTHEL TOKENS

Tokens exchangeable for services date from Roman times. The most notorious were those known as *spintriae*, denounced by the first-century poet Martial as "*lasciva numismata*", which scholars regard as brothel tokens or tickets of admission to spectacles of the grossest indecency, such as the Floralia, a licentious festival celebrated by prostitutes in honour of the goddess Flora. They were struck in brass and bore erotic motifs and Roman numerals. The largest hoard was discovered at Capraea, where the lecherous Emperor Tiberius held his orgies.

Brothel tokens, often with scenes of copulation as well as hearts and cupids, were also produced in Europe and the USA in the 19th and early 20th centuries, with naïve inscriptions such as "Good for a Night at Kate's Place".

ADMISSION TOKENS

Tokens in brass, silver or ivory were given to actors in the 18th and 19th centuries as complimentary tickets for use by their friends, while tokens valid for any performance during the season of a particular play were made of pewter, copper or brass and sold to patrons of the theatre. Special tokens, often in silver, were issued to those who subscribed to an entire season, or to shareholders and directors of a theatre company. They often had a panel or cartouche where the name of the patron and a box or seat number could be engraved.

Metallic admission tickets were also struck for the pleasure gardens such as Ranelagh or Vauxhall in 18th-century London. The idea was taken up by the Tivoli Gardens in Copenhagen and has extended in recent years to many other theme parks and tourist attractions. In this category may be included replicas of obsolete British coins (with contemporary dates) used at Ironbridge, Shropshire, birthplace of the Industrial Revolution, in the shops on the site, which charge old prices.

MILK TOKENS

Relics of an era when milk was delivered to doorsteps in glass bottles are the milk tokens used in Britain, Australia and New Zealand. These tokens, in various metals or coloured plastic, solved a problem that caused inconvenience and irritation to householders and milkmen alike – the theft of coins put in the empty bottles in payment for the next delivery. A petty thief raiding a whole row of doorsteps at night could

Below: A 25 øre token from a Danish amusement park.

net a tidy sum for a night's work. The most desirable tokens bear the name of the town and dairy (an example from St Kilda, Victoria, recently sold online for $60), but usually they are inscribed or stamped with the initials of the dairy or even the individual milkman, with numerals indicating the number of pints. Now that milk comes in disposable cartons, these tokens are a thing of the past – and very collectable.

TOKENS FOR SLOT MACHINES

Coin-operated public pay-phones were another tempting target for the street bandit and the cost of repairing the damaged equipment induced the authorities in many countries (mainly in continental Europe and Asia) to adopt a system whereby the public purchased tokens from a post office or tobacconist's kiosk. As these could not be exchanged for coins, there was no point in breaking into the machines to steal them. Furthermore, the actual sale price could be varied or increased without the expense of altering the slot machines. Similar tokens were later devised for other machinery that would normally have been activated by a coin in the slot, from parking meters to car-washing and laundry facilities.

Below: Transport tokens from Dunedin, New Zealand (top), and Paris (1921, middle), and a range of American bus or subway tokens (bottom).

Tobacco and Beer Tokens

These brass tokens advertising Samson cigarette tobacco (1987) and Hofmeister Lager not only promoted the products but also represented a small discount off the next purchase.

GAMING TOKENS

Called jetons (from the French *jeter*, "to throw") or counters, gaming tokens have been in existence since the 15th century. They are used as money substitutes in games of chance, although they originated as the metal discs used in medieval accountancy on a chequerboard or counting table (the "exchequer"). Brass counters with an imitation of the heraldic device of so-called Spade guineas, and with the royal titles replaced by such slogans as "In memory of the good old days" were used in early 19th-century Britain.

Gambling chips afford security to casinos as they have no real value until converted into cash. Although most modern chips are made in coloured plastic they may also be found in aluminium, brass or cupro-nickel. Small tokens, also known as pub checks, have been used for games of chance in public houses and entertainment arcades.

TRANSPORT TOKENS

In 1549, metal tokens were adopted at Regensburg to control bridge crossings and to represent a fee levied on those who wished to enter a walled town after the gates were closed for the night. The system spread to the USA in the 1790s, and Pennsylvania was the first state to introduce tollgate tokens on the turnpike highways.

In the 19th century the use of tokens extended to public transport of all kinds, from ferries to trams, buses and

Above: American Civil War soldiers being punished for gambling.

Below: Gambling tokens from the West Point Casino, Tasmania (1974) and the Palm Beach Club, London (1968).

subway systems. They were often given to employees of post offices or other public utilities, enabling them to travel free on company or municipal business. Most bear a civic or corporate emblem, but many modern examples feature vehicles. Associated with them are the tokens used at public lavatories or restrooms in bus and railway stations, where they are given only to bona fide passengers on presentation of a travel ticket. There are also numerous checks, tokens and tallies formerly used by railway companies, coal mines and market traders. Usually utilitarian in design, they are actively collected for their historical interest.

Below: A bronze sugar estate token of Mauritius with the head of Victoria.

COLLECTING COIN LOOKALIKES

Sooner or later every collector acquires one or more puzzle pieces, which look like coins and may even have a name or value inscribed on them but cannot be located in any of the standard catalogues. It seems obvious that such pieces must have had a valid reason for their existence, otherwise why would anyone have gone to all that trouble and expense to manufacture them?

BOGUS COINS

Imitation Spade guineas made of brass instead of gold have already been mentioned. They bore the profile of George III on one side and the royal arms in a spade-shaped shield on the other. Anyone who could read the motto inscribed on the coins – "In memory of the good old days" – would have no problem recognizing these pieces for gaming counters, but trouble arose when unscrupulous people passed them off as real gold guineas (worth 21 shillings, or £1.05) on unsuspecting (and illiterate) members of the public.

In the same category comes a brass piece that very closely resembles the gold sovereign current in the 1830s, with the monarch's effigy on the obverse and a reverse motif which, at first glance, might be mistaken for St George and the Dragon but which actually shows a crowned horseman. In place of the usual inscription are the words "To Hanover", which provide the clue to the identify of this piece. Under Salic Law, which insisted that a male heir must always take precedence,

Above: The obverse and reverse of mid-Victorian model coins struck by Joseph Moore of Birmingham, forerunners of today's bimetallic coins.

Queen Victoria could not succeed to the Hanoverian throne and her place was taken by her unpopular uncle, Prince George, Duke of Cumberland. It is believed that the "Cumberland Jack", as it is commonly known, was produced as a satirical piece, but it was often passed off as a genuine sovereign on the public.

MODEL COINS

At various times in 19th-century Britain the question of reducing the size and weight of the cumbersome copper or bronze coins was debated. The government was always reluctant to take such steps, clinging to the notion that even base metal coins should have an intrinsic metal value that was fairly close to the face value. It took well over a century for the authorities to abandon this notion and introduce the decimal coinage in small sizes, which weighed a fraction of their £sd predecessors.

As a possible solution to the problem, however, Joseph Moore, a Birmingham die-sinker and token manufacturer, produced a model coinage consisting of tiny bronze coins with a plug of silver in the centre. These model coins, portraying Queen Victoria, were intended to improve the coinage in general, as well as providing pieces whose intrinsic worth was the same as their circulating value. Similar bimetallic model coins were produced by Harry Hyams. These had a brass centre in a bronze surround, and ranged from the crown of 5 shillings (about the size of the modern 2 pence coin) to the halfpenny.

A tiny bronze coin was produced in 1887, with Victoria's profile on one side and St George and the Dragon on the other. The inscription "Jubilee Model Half Farthing" indicates its commemorative nature. Another such item is the diminutive silver piece portraying the infant Prince of Wales (later Edward VII), which was struck as a toy coin shortly after his birth in 1841. Model and miniature coins of this sort were popular as novelties in Christmas crackers during the 19th century.

Very tiny replicas of American coins are sold as souvenirs in the USA. At the other end of the spectrum are gigantic replica coins, often in the form of money-boxes or paperweights.

Spoof Coin

From 1966 until his death in 1987 Leonard Joseph Matchan was lessee of the tiny island of Brecqhou in the Channel Islands. As well as issuing stamps for a local postal service to Sark he created this spoof bronze coin, denominated "one knacker". As it was clearly never intended to be taken seriously, it did not render him liable to prosecution, unlike the owner of Lundy Island, whose coins of 1929 got him into trouble with the law and had to be withdrawn.

Below: Plastic play money from Hong Kong of the kind often used to teach children about different denominations.

Above: "Fantasy" Tibetan coins include this restrike of a quarter rupee by the Shanghai Mint (top) and a Sichuan fantasy dollar (bottom).

PLAY MONEY

Tiny replicas of current coins are produced in many countries for use as toy shop or dolls' money. Long ignored by numismatists, these pieces were sought out by collectors of dolls' house furniture and the like, but have now attracted the attention of coin collectors as well. Actual-size toy money, for teaching children arithmetic and the basics of shopping, is also collectable.

During the transitional period from sterling to decimal currency in Britain (1968–71) many types of instructional

Below: The publicity campaign that preceded British decimalization was aimed at businesses as well as the public, with measures taken, such as the release of 'play' coins, to ease the passing of the old currency system. In the event, the reforms were implemented within weeks.

money were produced, in plastic, metal or stout card, and these are now keenly collected as mementos of the greatest currency reform in Britain since Roman times. They were surpassed, however, by the instructional kits produced in the 12 European countries that adopted the euro in 2002. In many instances the kits, which included imitation coins, were supplied to every household.

FANTASY COINS

In 1925 a businessman, Martin Coles Harman, purchased Lundy, an island in the Bristol Channel, and proceeded to issue his own stamps. In 1929 he went so far as to issue his own coins, with his profile on one side and a puffin on the other. Because they were in the same metal, size and weight as the contemporary British penny and halfpenny, Harman was prosecuted under the Coinage Act of 1870, convicted and fined £5. The coins were withdrawn, but the dies were later used for an issue dated 1965, raising funds to preserve the island as a nature sanctuary.

In 1976, the self-styled Prince Leonard of the Hutt River Province (actually a sheep range in Western Australia) issued coins, from the aluminium 5 cents to the gold $100, which gained catalogue status, but not for long.

In Asia, the number of forged countermarks on Sichuan rupees and Tibetan coins during the early 20th century is such that a leading expert on Chinese coinage, Wolfgang Bertsch, self-published an entire volume dedicated to *Tibetan Fake Coins and Fantasy Countermarks* in 2003.

ELONGATES

Not really a coin lookalike but a novel way of converting a coin into a tourist souvenir or advertising piece, the elongate was invented by the American, Frank Brazzell, who also produced the machines to create them. The coin is

placed between two rollers, on one of which is engraved a motif. When the handle is turned the coin emerges in an elongated shape with the original obverse and reverse removed and a new image on one side. Thousands have been produced in the USA. Often termed elongate or 'flat' pennies, they feature a broad range of subjects, from publicity for local businesses to whole series on dinosaurs or baseball heroes. The idea eventually took root in Britain in 1981, when the law forbidding the defacement of coins was repealed. Elongates are now also popular souvenirs in France, Germany and other European countries, and often feature famous landmarks.

Above and left: A 2 euro plastic token and a German elongate from a 5 pfennig coin, as a souvenir of St Bartholomä's Church on the Königssee.

Below: A cased set of miniature replicas of American coins.

COLLECTING ERRORS AND VARIETIES

Serious collectors love to acquire items that are in some way off the beaten track or out of the ordinary. They look out for subtle differences in apparently similar coins, as well as various types of errors that arise in the course of manufacture but somehow get into general circulation, and sundry oddities such as coins hastily withdrawn from circulation because of a mistake in design.

DIE VARIATIONS

Right back in the days of the earliest hammered coinage, it soon became apparent that both the hammer and the anvil were liable to show signs of wear after the first few hundred coins had been struck. In many cases the designs engraved on the parts that actually struck the blanks could be sharpened up by re-engraving all or part of the surface. No matter how carefully this was done it gave rise to slight changes in the appearance of the coins.

As one side tended to wear out sooner than the other, scholars have often been able to trace the sequence of production by the combination of obverse and reverse impressions during the production of a particular coin. Hoards can often be a good source of large quantities of coins for such detailed studies.

This phenomenon is by no means confined to hammered coinage. Modern coins are produced in their millions, entailing the production of hundreds of dies. Theoretically, they should be identical but, inevitably, variations large and small tend to creep in. Sometimes these variations are quite deliberate, a prime example being the British gold sovereigns with shield

Left: This mis-struck Indian rupee of 1984 makes a curious sight, with its design around 75% off-centre.

Above: A cupro-nickel 1 baht coin of Thailand, with the design struck approximately 10 per cent off-centre.

reverse from 1863 to 1874, which bear tiny numbers engraved between the rose at the foot of the design and the knot tying the two laurel branches. All Shield-back sovereigns in this period should have a number ranging from 1 to 123 (though far fewer numbers were used in many years, while others may exist but have not yet been recorded). Some sovereigns of 1863 were issued without die numbers before the scheme started, and the same is true of 1874 coins after the practice was abandoned, but coins dated 1872 without die numbers are not uncommon. Conversely, a few sovereigns of 1863 have been discovered with the tiny numerals 827 impressed on the truncation of Queen Victoria's neck. Michael Marsh, the recognized authority on the gold sovereign, has recorded two examples with the die number 22 on the reverse and four without the die number, making the 827 coin one of the greatest rarities of British coinage.

Much more common are coins in the American series with the last digit of the date overstruck, a practice of the US Mint in the 19th century to change the date in line with federal law, which required coins to bear the actual year of striking. American coins also exhibit such die variations as large or small numerals. The coins of most countries feature die variants, ranging from slight changes in the actual design (such as the high and low horizons on British pennies) to the number of serrations in the edge, or the number of beads in the border of the rim.

Above: Victorian Shield-back sovereigns bearing die variation marks 36 and 52.

ERRORS

Accidents in manufacture give rise to some peculiar errors. A "brockage" is a coin with only one design, normal on one side and appearing incuse on the other. This occurs when a coin already struck adheres to the die and strikes the next blank to pass through the press. "Clash marks" are mirror-image traces on a coin struck by a pair of dies that have been damaged by having been struck together without a blank between them. Other mis-strikes occur

Below: Tibetan local government issues struck using different dies.

Above: A curved clip on a Sudanese 10 ghirsh coin of 1980.

Right: A British 10 pence struck by the Royal Mint in the scalloped collar of the Hong Kong $2, one of a batch shipped out to the colony, where the error was discovered.

when the dies are not properly aligned, and the design on one or both sides of the coin appears to be off-centre.

Such errors are ephemeral and are usually of little more than curiosity

---

Countermarked Dollars

At the end of the 18th century there was a severe shortage of silver coins in Britain. A large quantity of Spanish-American dollars (8 reales) had been captured and these were pressed into service, circulating as 5 shilling pieces and officially authorized by means of a countermark consisting of the bust of George III in an oval, or later octagonal, frame.

---

value. Much more interesting and desirable are hybrid coins, known to collectors as "mules", in which the obverse is not matched with its regular or official reverse. Mules have been recorded from Roman times, the obverse referring to one emperor and the reverse referring to a predecessor or another member of the imperial family. Accidental mules in recent times have resulted from the mixing of dies at mints where coins of several countries are being struck. This gives rise to such famous mules as the Coronation anniversary crowns with Ascension and Isle of Man dies, or 2 cent coins with Bahamas and New Zealand dies.

Restrikes of rare American coins have been detected in which the dated die has been paired with the wrong reverse, such as the 1860 restrike of the rare large cent of 1804.

Sometimes the wrong collar is used, the most spectacular examples being British 10 pence coins with a scalloped edge, which actually got into circulation in Hong Kong as $2 coins before the error was detected.

COUNTERMARKS

There have been many occasions on which marks have been applied to coins after they were issued, analogous to overprints on stamps. This is a normal procedure in cases where the value of the original coin has to be changed, and it was a widespread practice in Britain in 1800–4, when Spanish and other foreign coins were stamped with the effigy of George III to pass current for 5 shillings. The Bank of England even overstruck Spanish coins with a new obverse and Britannia on the reverse, but traces of the original design usually showed through.

Unofficial countermarks make an unusual sideline. Although it was a serious offence to deface coin of the realm it was common practice to engrave or strike pennies with a lover's initials. In some cases more elaborate motifs, such as entwined hearts, were stamped. In Northern Ireland, many British and

---

Above: Mules, pairing Italian and Russian rulers from a 20 lira coin of 1863 and 20 kopeks of 1867 (top) and colonial issues for Sierra Leone (obverse, bottom left) and Macao (right), mistakenly paired in the 1790s.

Irish coins of recent years have been countermarked by the IRA, UDA, UVF and other paramilitary factions, a curious memento of the "Troubles".

A particularly large and fascinating group consists of Spanish coins, or more often pieces of them, countermarked with values and the initials of various islands in the Caribbean, officially authorized as currency there, mainly in the 18th and early 19th centuries, before the introduction of a more regular coinage.

Below: Pennies of George III and George V with engraved or punch-marked letters, perhaps intended as love tokens. One has the incuse stamp of a broad arrow, an official government mark but here applied quite illegally.

COLLECTING PATTERNS, PROOFS AND EPHEMERA

Serious numismatists are not content with the coins that actually circulate, but also seek out pieces that trace the development of a coin from the earliest concept to the finished article, as well as the various versions produced by mints to supply the collectors' market, and even the packaging and promotional material associated with each new issue.

PATTERNS

Pieces resembling coins, prepared by the mint to the specifications of a new design or on the authorization of the coin-issuing authority, but differing in some respect from the coin that actually reaches the general public, are known as patterns. This category also includes pieces produced by mints when tendering for a coinage contract – an actual piece of metal being a much more effective sales tool than a sketch or a photograph.

Patterns may differ from the final coins as issued in the type or quality of metal used, but more often than not they differ in details of the design. Sometimes these differences may be

Below: A presentation folder from Estonia with a proof set of coins encased, 1999.

quite minor, such as the addition of some small detail, but they may be quite radical, or show entirely different motifs to those used for the issued coins. Patterns, especially if they exist in a sequence, are of particular use in illustrating the evolution of the coin.

Allied to them are the test pieces that occur when a new die is being tried out prior to going into actual production. These have a superficial resemblance to coins, in that they are usually struck on blanks of the correct weight and size, but the impression may vary from a mere ghostly outline to a nearly perfect image as the minter adjusts the machinery. Many test pieces, however, are known in lead or some other soft metal, pulled as the engraving of the dies is in progress, in order to make sure that no mistakes have arisen.

PROOFS

The die test pieces were, in fact, the true origin of proofs, but by the 19th century it had become standard mint practice to make impressions of coins on specially polished blanks for presentation purposes, and in more recent years this has become just another medium for selling coins to collectors.

Above: A 17th-century Christiania pattern silver strike of a gold coin.

Left: A pattern produced by VDM (a German manufacturer of coin blanks), with a reverse depicting the fortress of Altena, where the company is located.

The practice has now reached the point at which many deluxe coins are released only in proof form. They are undeniably very handsome but some purists are interested only in coins that actually get into general use, and some catalogues classify proofs of this kind as "non-circulating legal tender" (NCLT). One suspects that many of these beautiful pieces have never been accorded legal tender status.

PIEDFORTS

Derived from the French for "heavy or strong foot", the term "piedfort" denotes a coin struck with normal dies but on a blank of a much greater thickness than usual. The practice originated in France in the 15th century, when gold coins of twice or three times the normal thickness were struck for presentation to royalty, courtiers and foreign dignitaries. It spread to England in the reign of Henry VII. Examples of the gold sovereign, introduced in 1489, are known in double or treble weights. So far, only one of each has been recorded, and it is assumed that the king intended them as presentation pieces rather than high-value coins for general circulation.

This practice, long dormant, has been revived by the Royal Mint in recent years. The 50 pence coin, normally struck in cupro-nickel, was

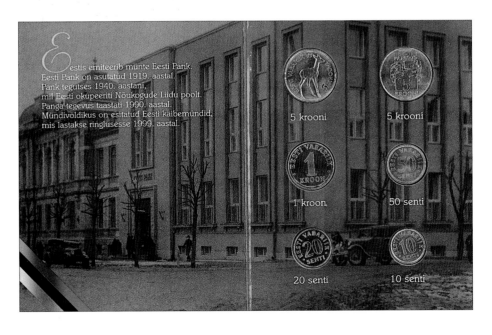

released in 1973 as a silver piedfort but only about 20 pieces were produced and they now command four-figure prices. Even the small 20 pence coin, introduced in 1982, was issued as a piedfort silver proof and this is now standard practice for pound coins (whose designs are changed each year) and commemorative 50 pence coins.

PACKAGING

Traditionally, proofs and year sets were tastefully packaged in leather cases lined with blue satin or plush. While this is still the case for the more expensive items, most mints have resorted to other forms of packaging, which are not only cheaper but more eye-catching. The vogue developed in the 1960s when year sets became fashionable. In

Below: A Dutch bronze pattern coin of William III tendering two possible reverse designs.

this era rigid plastic cases were adopted, the coins within them being inserted into stout cards printed with the national arms and salient details. In other examples the coins were merely encapsulated in thin plastic envelopes, although in some cases these were then inserted in paper envelopes with stiffener cards bearing descriptions of the coins. The current trend is towards much brighter, more colourful coin folders, which can be housed intact in coin albums. Different forms of packaging are often used, distinguishing between simple sets of circulating coins, sets in a superior finish but still in base metal, and the deluxe proofs in precious metals.

Two other recent developments seek to draw the sister hobbies of philately and numismatics closer together. Both originated in Germany, where coins and stamps have long been collected by the same people. The first is the philanumismatic cover, examples of which are now produced all over the world, while the second is the *Numisblatt*, which has so far made little headway beyond the country of origin. It consists of a stiff colour-printed card bearing stamps with special cancellations, with a coin encapsulated for good measure. *Numisblätter* are very similar to PNCs but are generally much larger and more decorative.

EPHEMERA

Serious collectors also watch out for the various pieces of ephemera associated with coins. These range from press cuttings and leaflets about new or forthcoming issues to mini-posters used by banks. Coins incorporated in premium giveaways or advertising gimmicks are also worth considering. Even chocolate packaged in metal foil stamped to resemble coins is collectable – assuming you can withstand the temptation to eat the contents.

Acts of Congress or other parliamentary bodies authorizing coins, as well as government reports on proposed changes, are also eminently collectable. Photographs and the

Above: A piedfort silver jeton depicting the assassination of William of Orange in 1584 (top) and a gold coronation jeton of Moscow.

original artists' thumbnail sketches reflecting the initial design concept for a coin are very desirable but are understandably rare. Such items are keenly fought over when they occasionally appear in the auction rooms.

Below: Collectable ephemera might even include hand-held beam balances and brass coin weights; such pocket balances were a must in the days of coin-clipping to check that coins were of full weight.

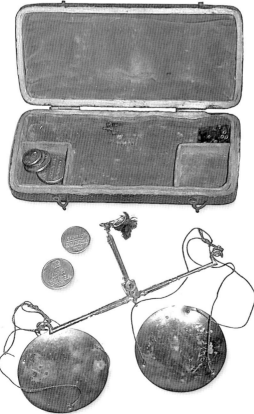

BUYING AND SELLING COINS

Although it is possible to form a collection from coins picked up in change or in the course of foreign travel, sooner or later you are more likely to want to start planning acquisitions in order to add to your collection in a meaningful way. There are several ways of acquiring new specimens: by exchange with fellow collectors, from dealers and by bidding at auction.

COIN CLUBS

All collectors inevitably accumulate material that is surplus to their requirements: such coins can very often be exchanged with fellow enthusiasts and new items added to the collection in return. If you are at all serious about your hobby, you will want to subscribe to a periodical devoted to the subject, and through it you can make contact with others through the small ads. You can also place an advertisement yourself stating what you have to offer and what you are looking for in exchange.

Most towns of any size have a coin club or numismatic society. Joining such a club gives you the chance to meet other collectors and swap coins. Your public library or museum will have information on clubs in the area, as will coin collectors' magazines. Many countries have a national numismatic society, perhaps with a website, which may be able to advise on local societies. Failing this, try an internet search.

Some clubs set aside time before or after each meeting for swapping, and in many cases one or more dealers will be in attendance. Others confine this activity to auctions once or twice a year. Apart from the chance to add to your collection, a coin club is the ideal venue to broaden your interests and improve your knowledge of coins.

Many of the larger numismatic societies host regular exhibitions and talks, and will be able to advise on the programme of events for the coming months. Some have extensive libraries of coins and other research facilities open to the public, or to members.

BUYING FROM DEALERS

A measure of how the hobby has grown in recent years is the increasing number of coin dealers operating in many European countries and elsewhere in the world, while the USA (which always had many more coin dealers than other countries) has retained its position in this respect.

Many dealers regularly take classified advertisements in coin magazines and are also fully listed in the various coin yearbooks and trade directories. A number of websites provide details of dealers who specialize in the coins of a particular country, region, period, denomination, or theme. The fact that the majority of dealers – from international companies specializing in tax-free gold to smaller-scale collectors offering information on their speciality and the opportunity to buy – now operate over the web means that the location of an outlet is much less important than in the past. As a result, it's possible to view images of and information about, and

Above: National numismatic bodies often promote clubs at local level and offer searchable, on-line directories.

purchase, coins from anywhere in the world, greatly increasing the possibilities for making new acquisitions.

BOURSES AND FAIRS

These radical changes in trading practice, combined with high overheads, have meant that the number of actual coin shops has dwindled, but at the same time buying coins by mail order has escalated dramatically and many dealers now send out regular lists to their clients. In addition, there are now many bourses, fairs and dealer circuits, giving collectors and dealers frequent opportunities to meet face to face.

Below: You may be fortunate enough to live in a town with a local coin shop, where you can purchase coins and kit.

Fairs and Forums

National societies such as the American Numismatic Assocation are extremely active at local level, organizing events ranging from coin marts to seminars on the role of coins in education and research. These occasions offer collectors a great opportunity to interact.

Annual fairs such as Coinex in London and the American Numismatic Association (ANA) World's Fair of Money or National Money Show provide opportunities for hundreds of collectors to exhibit and sell their wares. The United States is again the leader in this field, regularly hosting 10–20 high-profile coin shows per year in as many different states. The advantages of buying coins face to face or over the counter are obvious: you can examine the dealer's stock and be satisfied as to its condition before you buy.

AUCTIONS

The most important source of coins nowadays is the auction. Many of the finest collections and rarest coins are disposed of by auction, but this is also the place where bargains are to be found, and it may be the best method of buying a small collection intact to form the basis of a larger one.

London and New York continue to dominate the auction scene, with the largest and most prestigious salerooms, but there is also an increasing number of smaller auctions in provincial towns and cities. Much of the bidding at coin auctions is done by post, but there are so many pitfalls about buying in this way that it is advisable to get a coin dealer to bid on your behalf. Most dealers will do this for a small commission – it's simply a case of contacting a few to judge who can best work within the criteria you set. Most auction houses now add a buyer's premium to the sale price and this, with tax where applicable, can add considerably to the amount you have to pay. The general advice is, set your limit and stick to it.

SELLING COINS

Most collectors over-value their coins. Consequently, when they come to sell their collections, they are rapidly disillusioned and think that dealers are

Right: While expensive gold coins might be out of your reach, investing sparingly in a few choice, popular collectables will always reap returns in the long run.

trying to cheat them. There have also been times when coins were subject to speculation, usually when the stock market is low and traditional forms of investment are showing a poor yield. There are many horror stories of investors who burned their fingers at this end of the market. However, you should have confidence in those dealers who belong to a reputable trade association; you will find the appropriate logo in their display advertisements. You should remember that there is often quite a difference between a dealer's buying and selling prices – after all, dealers have to make a living and cover their overheads.

Some coins are in greater demand than others and it may be that your collection consists of material of which there is a more than adequate supply chasing a smaller demand. Condition is the biggest problem, as collectors – even very experienced ones – are sometimes over-optimistic about the state of their treasures. Dealers, who are handling coins every day, develop a keen eye for condition and are quick to spot the flaws and blemishes that collectors often overlook, but which materially affect the value of coins.

Dealers will at least make you an offer for spot cash, and such transactions are swift. Selling by auction may net you a higher return in the long run, but several months can elapse between consigning coins to the saleroom and

Above: World coin and medal dealer Baldwin's was established by the English numismatist Arthur Henry Baldwin in 1901. He began by selling coins from his home in Plumstead, London, before setting up shop with his three sons.

the actual auction, with a further wait for the proceeds, less the auctioneer's commission. In fact, despite the existence of dealers and auctioneers, and the rapid growth of on-line trading, many collectors still prefer the long-established method of selling direct to other collectors. Most clubs provide opportunities for this, and even arrange meetings for buying.

ON-LINE NUMISMATICS

The IT revolution has changed everyone's life in many different ways, so it is not surprising that it has also had a major impact on numismatics, bringing fellow collectors closer together, offering an unrivalled tool for research and, above all, for buying and selling coins on-line. Home computers with broadband connections are becoming increasingly commonplace. Indeed, the time is not far off when these facilities will be as accessible to the public as is the telephone or television today.

DEALERS' WEBSITES

Only a few years ago, websites set up by coin dealers were more or less a complete novelty. Only about a dozen dealers and auctioneers in Britain offered this facility, and, it must be admitted, their sites were decidedly patchy. All that has changed. Every coin dealer is now on-line – he or she could not survive in the numismatic trade otherwise – and their web pages are generally highly professional and easy to follow, usually with excellent

Below: Part of the fun of round-the-clock on-line bidding is waiting to see whether you have been successful.

links. You can view coins on screen in great detail, and buy in seconds with a click of a mouse.

SEARCHING FOR COINS

Type the word "coins" into an internet search engine, for example, and you might be confronted with no fewer than 20 million different options. It would of course take many years to browse through these: the term is just far too vague. More useful, though still very general, search terms might include "old coins", "US coins", "rare coins" or "gold coins".

As a rule, global search engines will push larger or sponsored sites to the fore, which is likely to include wholesalers advertising a vast range of goods besides coins, such as Amazon or Yahoo Shopping. National mints also compete for collector's attentions, as well as the tourist market, many with sites offering a digital 'tour' through the mint, and the chance to buy the latest issues.

To narrow down the search, you can try a more specific subject. Keying in "Crusader coins", which is a relatively esoteric topic, might still bring up as many as 47,000 sites. A refined search for the coinage of Baldwin II, King of

Jerusalem, will pull up far fewer sites, so the chances are that you would be able to find out everything you would ever need to know on that topic.

Naturally, as with any internet search, you need to be discriminating about what you find and verify its reliability (which is often possible by cross-checking factual material with other websites), but there is now a great deal of high quality numismatic information on the internet.

CONTACTING OTHERS

CoinTalk, the discussion forum that is likely to pop up near the top of any numismatic search, is designed as a non-esoteric medium for debate "where Numismatists, Collectors, Dealers and Novices [can] gather to discuss Coins". As soon as you open this site you are confronted with a bewildering array of choices. On the left side are links to a large number of dealers' websites, including "a comprehensive A to Z to reputable coin dealers" provided by www.shopperuk.com, which, in turn, opens up a whole world of reputable coin traders.

To get into the forum itself, you have to register, but this takes only a few minutes and you are then free to join in the discussion on any coin topic imaginable. Typical topics under discussion include "What's it worth?" (a perennial question), errors on coins, ancient coins, US coins, world coins, and so on. In other words, it is a worldwide network of fellow enthusiasts. Topics of discussion such as "Variety Nickels" might drawn in hundreds of threads and posts as collectors discuss the minutiae of dates, mint-marks and die variants in this ever-popular American coin. Coin forums are also an excellent place to post an advertisement about hard-to-find coins – you are certain to have a response from a collector somewhere in the world who has recently made a similar purchase, or who knows of a specialist dealer. The numismatic grapevine is a valuable entity for collectors seeking to make new acquisitions or simply to learn more and, though still in its infancy, the potential for growth is huge.

BUYING ONLINE

As noted previously, most coin dealers now maintain websites, with detailed descriptions and high-resolution images allowing you to make purchases safely from anywhere in the world.

There are also many on-line auction sites on the internet, but the largest and best-known is eBay, where many of the coins on sale are offered by collectors themselves. This is often the medium of choice for buyers and sellers alike, because of the breadth of the audience it attracts and because, despite its ever-growing scope, it remains dedicated to secure shopping. Refining your bidding technique is part of the fun; rather like a gambler, it is often wise not to show your hand and place a serious bid until the final stages of the auction.

The larger auction sites usually offer a facility whereby you can view an enlarged picture in which any knocks and scratches would soon be apparent. Some collectors tell salutary tales about images being doctored and sharpened

International marketplace

Described as the world's on-line marketplace, eBay was founded in 1995 by Pierre Omidyar of Echo Bay, California, who was convinced that the internet could be used as a tool for buying and selling. The site has revolutionized the coin trade, with about 300,000 lots of coins of all periods and countries on offer at any moment.

---

up, so that a coin that appears on screen as "brilliant uncirculated" turns out to be no more than about "very fine", but this does not seem to be the general experience. Moreover, security is tightening. Ebay's "Code of Conduct for Selling Coins and Paper Money", published on its website and created in conjunction with leading numismatic bodies such as the ANA, aims to stamp out the passing off of reproductions and copies as the genuine article by effectively blackballing any unscrupulous sellers who do so.

The biggest problem with the global nature of online auctions can be that, for a particular coin you are interested in, the closing time may be 3.30 p.m. on the other side of the world, which happens to be the middle of the night where you are. You can either leave a high bid, in the hope that you outbid rival bidders, or set your alarm clock and follow the actual bidding to a nail-biting conclusion in the small hours.

When buying coins in your own country, you can usually send a personal cheque through the post, but the use of PayPal is pretty well mandatory for purchases from abroad. It is easy to register, and thereafter purchases in American or Australian dollars, euros, or any other currency are automatically

Above: Powerful digital cameras enable razor-sharp images of coins to be posted to dealers' websites. If you are hoping to sell your own coins in this way, remember that sharp images bolster confidence among collectors.

translated into your own and debited to your credit card – a painless and very fast process.

COIN PROFILES

Vendors' descriptions on auction sites are not always as helpful as they might be. Some wax lyrical about the origins of the coins but omit the important details. Larger sites do try to steer would-be sellers in the right direction by including essential questions about the item(s) as part of the formulation of an on-line profile or account. Ultimately, however, the success of a transaction largely comes down to the buyer having a clear idea of what they want, and confidence in the sale. In this respect, it is very important that on-line vendors scan the coins intended for sale at as high a resolution as possible. Serious, potential buyers will be frustrated by images scanned at 100dpi or less, as these make it impossible to judge whether the coins on offer really live up to their professed grading.

GLOSSARY

Some of the more commonly used terms are given below.

Accolated *see* **conjoined**.

Adjustment The filing down of a blank to reduce it to the correct weight before striking, revealed by file marks on the surface.

Ae Abbreviation of *aes* (Latin, "bronze"), used to denote copper, brass or bronze.

Aes grave (Latin, "heavy bronze") Heavy coinage of the Roman Republic from 269 BC.

Aes rude (Latin, "rough bronze") Irregular lumps of bronze used as money before the adoption of regular coinage, *c.* 400 BC.

Aes signatum (Latin, "signed bronze") Regular bars or ingots cast to a standard weight, stamped to guarantee their weight, 289–269 BC.

Alliance coinage Coins struck by two or more states in conjunction.

Alloy Mixture of metals, such as bronze (copper and tin).

Altered Deliberately changed, usually to increase the value of a coin (such as changing a common date to a rare one by filing one of the digits).

Aluminium Lightweight silver-coloured metal used for coins of low denominations.

Aluminium-bronze Durable, gold-coloured alloy of aluminium and copper.

Amulet Coin whose design confers talismanic properties, often pierced and worn to ward off evil spirits. *See also* **touchpiece**.

Anepigraphic coin Coin with no inscription.

Angel Gold coin named for its image of Archangel Michael, first used in France in 1340 and introduced to England in 1465, with a value of 6 shillings and 8 pence.

Annealing Process of heating and cooling metal to relieve stresses before it is processed.

Annulet Small circle used as an ornament or spacing device in inscriptions.

Antoniniani Roman imperial coins named after the emperor Caracalla (Marcus Aurelius Antoninus) in whose reign they were first minted.

Ar Abbreviation of *argentum* (Latin, "silver").

Assay Test to determine the fineness of precious metal.

Attribution Identification of a coin by such data as the issuer, date, reign, mint or denomination.

Au Abbreviation of *aurum* (Latin, "gold").

Barbarous Descriptive of coins struck by Celtic and Germanic tribes in imitation of Greek or Roman coins.

Base metal Non-precious metal or an alloy containing neither gold nor silver.

Bath metal Inferior bronze alloy used at Bath, England, for casting cannon, but also employed by William Wood of Bristol to produce tokens for Ireland and colonial America.

Beading Border of raised dots round the rim of a coin.

Billon Alloy of copper with less than 50 per cent silver.

Bimetallic Made of two different metals or alloys; such coins usually have a centre in one metal and outer ring in another.

Bimetallism Descriptive of coinage consisting of coins in two different metals with a fixed ratio between them, such as gold and silver or silver and bronze.

Bit (1) Segment of a coin that has been cut up in order to circulate at half or one quarter the value of the entire coin. (2) Nickname of the 1 real piece that circulated in North America in the 17th and 18th centuries, worth one eighth of a dollar, or 12½ cents.

Blank Disc of metal cut or punched out of a strip or sheet, on which a coin is struck. Also known as a flan or planchet.

Blundered inscription (1) Jumbled lettering in inscriptions on barbarous coins, reflecting the illiteracy of the makers copying Greek or Roman coins. (2) Unreadable inscription as a result of a mis-strike.

Bon pour (French, "good for") Inscription on 1920s French tokens used during a shortage of legal tender coins.

Bourse Area in a coin exhibition where dealers sell their wares.

Bracteate (from Latin *bractea*, a thin piece of metal) Coin struck on such a thin blank that the image impressed on one side shows through on the other.

Brass Alloy of copper and zinc.

Brockage Mis-struck coin with only one design, normal on one side and incuse on the other, caused when a struck coin clings to the die and strikes the next blank to pass through the press.

Bronze Alloy of copper and tin.

Bullet money Globular pieces of silver with impressed marks, used as currency in Thailand from the 14th century until 1904.

Bullion Precious metal whose value is reckoned solely by its weight and fineness.

Bullion coin Coin struck in precious metal, now usually with an inscription giving its weight and fineness, whose value fluctuates according to the market price of the metal.

Buyer's premium Percentage of the purchase price at auction paid by the winning bidder to the auction house.

Carat (US karat) Term used to denote the fineness of gold, being 1/24 of the whole. Thus 22 carat gold is .916 fine.

Cartwheel Nickname of the British penny and 2 pence copper coins of 1797, weighing respectively 1oz/28.35g and 2oz/56.7g, with raised rims resembling cartwheels.

Cased set Set of coins in mint condition, packaged by the mint.

Cash (from Portuguese *caixa* and Tamil *kacu*, a small coin) Cast circular coins in copper or bronze with a square central hole, used as subsidiary coinage in China.

Cast coins Coins made by pouring molten metal into moulds, rather than by striking discs of metal with dies.

Clad Descriptive of a coin with a core of one metal covered with a layer or coating of another.

Clash marks Mirror-image traces found on a coin struck with dies that have been damaged by having been previously struck together without a blank between them.

Clipping Removing slivers of silver or gold from the edge of coins, an illegal but widespread practice until the 1660s, when milled coins began to be struck

with grained edges.

Cob Irregularly shaped silver piece sliced from a bar of silver and crudely stamped for use in Spanish America in the 16th to 18th centuries.

Coin Piece of metal marked with a device and issued by a government for use as money.

Coin weight Piece of metal of exactly the weight of a known coin, used to check weight and fineness of matching coins.

Collar Ring within which the obverse and reverse dies operate to restrict the spread of the blank between them; it is often engraved with an inscription or pattern that is impressed on the edge of the coin.

Commemorative Coin struck to celebrate a historic anniversary or personality or publicize an event.

Conjoined portrait Obverse portrait with two heads or busts in profile, facing the same direction and overlapping. Also known as accolated or jugate.

Convention money Coins struck by neighbouring states and mutually acceptable; specifically the issues of Austria and Bavaria, which spread to other German states in the early 19th century.

Copper (1) Metal widely used for subsidiary coinage for more than 2500 years, usually alloyed with tin to make bronze, but also alloyed with nickel or silver. (2) Nickname for small denomination coins.

Coppernose Nickname derived from the debased English silver shillings of Henry VIII because the silver tended to wear off the king's nose, the highest point of the obverse.

Counter Piece resembling a coin but actually intended for use on a medieval accountancy board or in gambling.

Counterfeit Imitation of a coin for circulation, intended to deceive the public and defraud the state.

Countermark Punch mark applied to a coin to change its value or authorize its circulation in a different state.

Crockards Debased imitations of English silver pennies, produced in the Low Countries and imported into England in the late 13th century.

Crown gold Gold of 22 carat (.916) fineness, so called because it was first used in England in 1526 for the gold crown; it remains the British standard.

Cupellation (Latin *cupella*, little cup) Refining process used to separate gold and silver from lead and other impurities in a bone ash pot called a cupel; used in assaying to determine the fineness of precious metals.

Cupro-nickel (US copper-nickel) Alloy of copper and nickel.

Currency Money of all kinds, including coins, paper notes, tokens and other articles, passing current in general circulation.

Current Descriptive of coins and paper money in circulation.

Cut money Coins cut into smaller pieces to provide proportionately smaller values for general circulation.

Debasement Reduction of a coin's precious metal content.

Decimal currency Currency system in which the basic unit is divided into 10, 100 or 1000 subsidiary units.

Demonetization Withdrawal of coins from circulation, declaring them to be worthless.

Denomination Value given to a coin or note of paper money.

Device Term derived from heraldry for the pattern or emblem on a coin.

Die Hardened piece of metal bearing the mirror or wrong-reading image of a device, used to strike one side of a blank.

Die break Raised line or bump in a relief image caused by a crack in the die.

Dodecagonal Twelve-sided.

Dump Coin struck on a very thick blank.

Eagle US gold coin with an American eagle obverse and a face value of $10, circulating until 1933.

Ecclesiastical coins Coins struck under the authority of an archbishop or other prelate, prevalent in the Middle Ages and surviving in coins of the Papacy.

Edge The side of a coin, perpendicular to the obverse and reverse surfaces, which may be plain, inscribed or grained.

Edge inscription Lettering on the edge of coins designed to prevent clipping.

Edge ornament Elaboration of the graining on milled coins designed as a security device.

Effigy Portrait or bust on the obverse of a coin.

Electrum Naturally occurring alloy of gold and silver prevalent in the ancient coins of the Mediterranean region; it was also known as white gold.

Encased money Stamps enclosed in small metal discs and used in lieu of coins during the American Civil War and in Europe during and after World War I.

Engraving Technique of cutting designs and inscriptions in dies used for striking coins.

Epigraphy Study of inscriptions engraved in stone or metal, usually to determine the date and provenance of an artefact so inscribed.

Erasure Removal of the title or effigy of a ruler from coinage issued posthumously, notably in Roman coins of Caligula and Nero.

Error Mistake in the design or production of a coin.

Exergue Bottom segment of the face of a coin, usually divided from the rest of the field by a horizontal line and often containing the date or value.

Face Obverse or reverse surface of a coin.

Face value Value of the denomination applied to a coin, distinct from its intrinsic value.

Facing Descriptive of a portrait facing to the front instead of in profile.

Fantasy Piece purporting to be a coin but either emanating from a non-existent country or never authorized by the country whose name is inscribed on it.

Field Flat part of a coin between the legend and effigy or other raised parts of the design.

Flan *see* **blank**.

Forgery Unauthorized copy or imitation, produced primarily to deceive collectors.

Frosting Matt finish used for the high relief areas of proof coins to contrast with the polished surface of the field.

Globular Descriptive of a coin struck on a very thick dump with convex sides.

Gold Precious metal used for coins since the 7th century BC.

Grade Description of the condition of a collectable coin for the purposes of valuation and trade.

Graining Pattern of close vertical ridges around the edge of milled coins, originally devised to eliminate the fraudulent practice of clipping. Also known as reeding or milling.

Gun money Emergency Irish coinage of 1689–91 struck from gunmetal by the deposed James II in order to pay and supply his troops during the Williamite or Jacobean War.

Hammered Descriptive of coins struck by hand, using a hammer to impress the dies.

Hoard Group of coins buried or hidden in the past.

Holed coin (1) Coin minted with a central hole. (2) Coin pierced after striking, to wear as jewellery or a talisman.

Hub Right-reading metal punch used to strike working dies.

Incuse Descriptive of an impression that cuts into the surface of a coin.

Ingot Piece of precious metal, cast in a mould and stamped with its weight and fineness.

Intrinsic value Net value based on the metal content of a coin, as opposed to its nominal or face value.

Iron Metal used in primitive currency such as the spits of ancient Greece, and for emergency coinage in both World Wars.

Jeton (from French *jeter*, to throw) Alternative term for **counter**.

Jugate (from Latin *jugum*, yoke) Alternative term for **conjoined**.

Key date The rarest date in a long-running series.

Klippe Coin struck on a square or rectangular blank hand-cut from sheet metal, originally in a time of emergency.

Laureate Descriptive of a design incorporating a laurel wreath, either adorning the brows of a ruler or enclosing the value.

Legal tender Coin declared by law to be current money.

Legend Inscription on a coin.

Long cross coinage English pennies first issued by Henry III, on which the arms of the cross on the reverse reached to the rim.

Lustre Sheen or bloom on the surface of an uncirculated coin.

Maundy money Set of small silver pennies distributed by the British sovereign to the poor on Maundy Thursday (preceding Good Friday), a medieval custom still enacted. Ordinary coins were originally used but special 1, 2, 3 and 4 pence coins were first minted in 1822.

Milling Mechanical process for the production of coins, in use from the 16th century.

Mint Establishment in which coins are produced. Also used as a grading term.

Mint set Coins still enclosed in the package or case issued by the mint.

Mint-mark Mark on a coin identifying the mint at which it was struck.

Mirror surface Highly polished, flawless surface of the field of a proof coin.

Mis-strike Coin on which the impression of the die has been struck off-centre.

Moneyer Mint official in pre-industrial era responsible for striking coinage of legal weight and quality.

Mule Coin whose obverse and reverse designs are wrongly matched. Can be comprised of different denominations or even separate foreign currencies.

Nickel Base metal used extensively in coinage as a substitute for silver, frequently alloyed with copper to make cupro-nickel.

Non-circulating legal tender Coins that, though technically valid for use, do not circulate in practice (such as silver and gold commemoratives). Abbreviated to NCLT.

Numismatics (from Latin *numisma*, coin) The study and collection of paper money, coins and medals.

Obverse "Heads" side of a coin.

Off-metal Descriptive of a coin struck in a metal other than that officially authorized.

Overdating Method of changing a date without the expense of engraving an entirely new die. One or more digits are altered by superimposing other numerals using a punch.

Overstrike Coin produced when a previously struck coin is substituted for a blank, on which traces of the original design remain.

Patina Surface quality acquired as a result of environmental interaction over time, such as the oxidation of metal.

Pattern Design piece prepared by a mint for approval by the issuing authority, not actually put into production. Patterns may differ from issued coins in metal or minor details, but many bear designs quite different from those eventually adopted.

Pellet Raised circular ornament, sometimes used as a spacing device in the inscription.

Pieces of eight Nickname for Spanish silver 8 real coins.

Piedfort (US piefort) Coin struck on a blank of two or three times the normal weight and thickness.

Pile Lower die bearing the obverse motif, the opposite of the trussel.

Planchet *see* **blank**.

Platinum Precious metal first used for coins in Russia in 1819 and occasionally in recent years for proof coins.

Plate money Large, cumbersome copper plates used as money in Sweden, 1643–1768.

Privy mark Secret mark incorporated in a coin design as a security device or to identify the particular die used.

Profile Side portrait often used on the obverse of coins.

Proof Originally a trial strike but in recent years a coin struck to a very high standard, often in precious metals.

Punch Piece of hardened metal bearing a design or lettering used to impress a die or a coin.

Recoinage Process of recalling and demonetizing old coins, which are then melted down and made into new coins.

Reeding *see* **graining**.

Relief Raised parts of the design.

Restrike Coin produced from the original dies, but long after the period in which they were current.

Reverse "Tails" side of a coin, usually featuring arms, the value or a pictorial design.

Rim Raised border around the outside of a coin's face.

Scissel Clippings of metal left after a blank has been cut; sometimes a clipping accidentally adheres to the blank during striking, producing a crescent-shaped flaw.

Scyphate (from Greek *scypha*, skiff or small boat) Cup-shaped, used to describe Byzantine concave coins.

Sede vacante (Latin, "vacant see") Inscription used on issues of ecclesiastical mints between the death of a prelate and the election of his successor.

Series All the issues of a coin of one denomination, design and type, including modifications and variations.

Short-cross coinage English pennies on which the arms of the reverse cross fell far short of the rim.

Siege money Emergency currency issued under siege.

Silver Precious metal widely used for coinage from the 6th century BC onward.

Slabbing Method of encapsulating a coin permanently, particularly in a rectangular plastic case, to prevent deterioration.

Specie (Latin, "in kind") Money in the form of coins, especially of precious metals.

Steel Metal refined and tempered from iron and used in a stainless or chromed version for coinage since 1939. Copper-clad steel is now extensively used in place of bronze.

Tin Metal used for small coins in Malaysia, Thailand and the East Indies, and in British halfpence and farthings (1672–92). It is more usually alloyed with copper to form bronze.

Token Coin-like piece of metal, plastic or card issued by merchants, local authorities or other organizations, often during periods when government coinage is in short supply, but also produced extensively as a substitute for money.

Touchpiece Coin kept as a lucky charm and often pierced to wear

as jewellery, notably the English gold angel, which was believed to cure or ward off scrofula, a skin disease known as the King's Evil.

Trade coin Coin produced for use outside the country of origin as part of international trade, such as British and American trade dollars.

Truncation Stylized cut at the base of the neck of a portrait, sometimes the site of a mint-mark, the engraver's initials or a die number.

Trussel Upper die used in hammered coinage bearing the reverse design, the opposite of the pile.

Type A major variety of a series of coins.

Type set Set comprising one coin of each type in a series.

Uniface Coin with a device on one side only.

Vis-à-vis (French, "face-to-face") Descriptive of a double portrait in which the two heads face each other.

White gold Ancient term for **electrum**, which differs from the modern definition.

Year set Set of coins produced annually by a mint, usually containing a specimen of each coin issued by the mint during the year.

Zinc Metal alloyed with copper to produce brass; zinc-coated steel was also widely used in Europe during both World Wars.

GRADING TERMINOLOGY

You will find below the various terms given in catalogues and dealers' lists to denote the perceived state, or 'grade', of a coin, with the higher grades given first.

Fleur de Coin (FDC) or **Brilliant Uncirculated (BU** or **B. Unc.)** Denotes coins in the very finest possible condition with full original lustre, no surface marks or edge knocks. Usually reserved for descriptions of proof and de luxe coins.

Uncirculated (Unc.) The highest grade applicable to coins struck by high-speed presses for general circulation. These coins should have full original lustre, which may have darkened with age to produce an attractive patina. Otherwise the surface should be flawless.

Extremely Fine (EF) Indicates a coin in virtually pristine condition but showing slight signs of handling. It should have every detail of the engraving clearly delineated but will have lost some of its original lustre.

Very Fine (VF) Coins show slight evidence of wear on the highest points of the design, notably the hair on portraits and the ridge at the truncation of the bust. In modern coins this is the lowest grade for practicable purposes and to purchase a coin in any lesser condition would be a waste of money. Dealers do not normally offer modern coins in lower grades unless they are very scarce. Older material, however, may be acceptable.

Fine (F) To the uninitiated such a coin may seem perfectly acceptable, but look closely and you will see that the higher points of the design are worn smooth and the lettering is noticeably thicker and less clearly defined, especially in the serifs (the little spurs on capitals) which may have all but disappeared.

Very Good (VG) A misuse of language as a coin with this description would be in pretty poor condition. In such coins little of the fine detail will be present and the overall impression would be blurred and worn.

Good (G) Now means the complete opposite. A coin in this state would be worn smooth all over and the date would be just readable. For that reason alone collectors will keep such a coin if a particular year is so scarce that the chances of finding a better

specimen might be remote.

Lower grades, such as **Fair**, **Mediocre** and **Poor** have almost vanished from the scene and would only be considered if the coin was seldom available in a better condition. These terms are usually reserved for medieval coins which have been clipped or have irregular shapes with chunks missing – which is, in fact, a not uncommon situation for many coins from the 10th to 16th centuries. Also included in these categories are coins which have been pierced for wear as pendants, the only exception in this case being the gold angels of medieval Europe, which were believed to guard the bearer against disease, and which are still highly valued by auctioneers and collectors.

INDEX

PICTURE ACKNOWLEDGEMENTS

The publishers would like to thank A H Baldwin and Sons Ltd, London for their kind assistance in supplying a substantial number of images from their photographic archive for use in this book.

All images in the book were supplied by Dr James Mackay and A H Baldwin and Sons Ltd, London unless otherwise indicated below.
(Note: t= top; b = bottom; l = left; r= right)

2: The Mary Evans Picture Library; 6bl: The Art Archive/Museo della Civilta Romana Rome/Dagli Orti; 6br: The Art Archive/Musée du Louvre Paris/Dagli Orti (A); 8tr (in panel): The Mary Evans Picture Library; 8bl: The Mary Evans Picture Library; 9t: The Mary Evans Picture Library; 11m: The Mary Evans Picture Library; 9b: Mary Evans/Meledin Collection; 10t: The Art Archive/Dagli Orti; 10bl: The Mary Evans Picture Library; 13tl: The Mary Evans Picture Library; 13tr: The Art Archive/Victoria and Albert Museum London/Eileen Tweedy; 15br The Art Archive/Archaeological Museum Naples/Dagli Orti (A); 16b: The Art Archive/Rheinische Landesmuseum Trier/Dagli Orti; 18t: The Art Archive/ Bodleian Library Oxford; 19bl: The Mary Evans Picture Library; 21tr; The Mary

Evans Picture Library; 22t: The Art Archive/Sienese State Archives/Dagli Orti (A); 24br: The Art Archive/Bodleian Library Oxford; 28tr: The Mary Evans Picture Library; 30bl: The Art Archive/American Museum Madrid; 32br: The Art Archive/Musée Carnavalet Paris/Dagli Ortii; 34bl: The Art Archive/Musée du Louvre Paris/Harper Collins Publishers; 35tr: The Art Archive/Ministry of Education Tokyo/Laurie Platt Winfrey; 36bl: The Art Archive/Templo Mayor Library Mexico/Dagli Orti; 40br: The Art Archive/Museo Correr Venice/Dagli Orti; 41t: The Art Archive/Dagli Orti (A); 44tr: Mary Evans Picture Library; 44bl: The Mary Evans Picture Library; 45: All images on this page appear courtesy of the Perth Mint, Western Australia; 46bl: Courtesy of the Perth Mint, Western Australia; 47tl: Courtesy of the Perth Mint, Western Australia; 48tr: The Mary Evans Picture Library; 49bl: Courtesy of the Perth Mint, Western Australia; 49br: The Mary Evans Picture Library; 54tr: The Art Archive/Archaeological Museum Ferrara/Dagli Orti (A); 56t: (coin of Holy Roman Emperor Charles V): The Art Archive/Dagli Orti (A); 57bl: The Mary Evans Picture Library; 57br: The Mary Evans Picture Library; 61br: Courtesy of the Perth Mint, Western Australia; 62m (Discover

Australia collector's folder) courtesy of the Perth Mint, Western Australia; 63bl: Courtesy of the Perth Mint, Western Australia; 65tr: Web page reproduced by permission of the American Numismatic Association; 66tr: Web page reproduced by permission of the American Numismatic Association; 67br (Discover Australia coins): Courtesy of the Perth Mint, Western Australia; 69tr: The Mary Evans Picture Library; 70br (in panel): Courtesy of the Perth Mint, Western Australia; 73t: The Art Archive/Culver Pictures; 76br: Courtesy of the Perth Mint, Western Australia; 79tr (in panel): Courtesy of the Perth Mint, Western Australia; 80bl: The Mary Evans Picture Library; 81tr: The Mary Evans Picture Library; 89tr: Web page reproduced by permission of the American Numismatic Association; 89bl (in panel): Image reproduced by permission of the American Numismatic Association; 90tr: Web page reproduced by permission of the American Numismatic Association.

Paul Baker supplied the following images of coins:
77mr (Iranian rial showing mosque); 82bl (Hong Kong 'play money'; 83tr (Euro plastic token); 83mr (elongate coin); 85tl (curved clip on Sudanese coin).